The Girls Who Refused to Quit

The
Girls Who
Refused
to Quit

A Welford Publishing Collaboration

Published in 2020 by Welford Publishing
Copyright © Cassandra Farren 2020
ISBN: Paperback 978-1-9162671-0-7
Cassandra Farren has asserted her right to be identified as the author of
this Work in accordance with the Copyright, Designs and Patents Act
1988.

Front cover photograph © Guille Álvarez
Front cover design © Jen Parker
Author photograph © Kate Sharp Photography 2018
Editor Christine McPherson

A catalogue for this book is available from the British Library.

Poem written by Cassandra

Your questions have no answers,
You feel lost, alone, and afraid.
Your head is spinning endlessly
As life passes in a daze.

It's time to trust your instincts,
Allow your pain and the darkness to fade.
Your lessons are ready to unfold now,
They will guide you day by day.

No anger or regrets will consume you
As you find the strength to move on.
Your voice and the strength within you
Were with you all along.

Hold your head high, live life on your terms,
You can do this, it's time to commit.
Know that you're worthy, take one step at a time

From
   The Girls Who Refused to Quit

One Woman's Journey

Rachel Jewell

8th December 2004

No, don't go, don't leave me, please! I can't do this, don't leave me here. Please don't leave me! My silent screams go unheard as his hand leaves mine, his tears fall whilst doubt creases his features. Is it his fault? Is it mine? With the turning of my husband's back, everything that had happened in my life to date was magnified to this one moment. My life as I knew it collapsed.

'Come on, Rachel, let's take you upstairs to the nurses' station,' says the admissions woman as she walks me through a spectacular atrium, complete with an indoor fishpond surrounded by imposing fragrant flower displays, which sharply awaken my senses.

Two nurses greet me, passing sympathetic smiles between them. One takes a blood sample, the other pops pills into a plastic pot, saying, 'Take these. Have you brought any razors, scissors, aerosols or needles in with you today? We need to take your mobile phone.'

I'm not sure if I'm shaking with fear or shivering from the December temperatures, yet pure ice has replaced the blood in my veins. *What the hell is happening to me? Please make it stop. I can't breathe, I can't function. I cannot understand this situation. I am going to pass out.* I fall onto the chair, mute.

'Let's show you to your room,' suggests the blonde-haired nurse.

We walk along a corridor to the end door. Somehow, my brain processes that this old country house is beautiful, dated and slightly battered by the more recent life that it has held within its walls over the last 20 years or so. We enter a large room, semi-partitioned, with four single beds. Mine appears to be the bed in the corner. My phone and purse already taken from me, the nurse proceeds to unpack my case, running her hands through the lining, then turns out my coat pockets. She leaves. I sit down on the bed. Alone. I am in full blown despair. I am totally and utterly ashamed. I am broken.

'Rachel.' A man comes into the room; he says he is a counsellor.

'There is no lock on my room, there are other people sleeping in this room. I am not safe here. I cannot stay here, don't you understand?' I sob.

His soothing tone is cold comfort.

We go downstairs and outside to a first-floor balcony for a cigarette, and the most spectacular views of the countryside greet me. After a split second of peace, I turn away from the view to see other people – some look beaten, vacant; others loud, swearing, and spitting. There is a woman around my age, drunk, laughing, smiling, still oblivious to the horror that is my reality. She says, 'Hi, I'm Juliette,' whilst dancing around me. I think I may like her. I feel a sadness for her that she will soon sober up.

A bell rings; it's deafening; it's dinner time. My senses ache. Every scrape of every chair, every piece of cutlery, plate, and utterance from the thirty-plus people, sends excruciating pain through every nerve in my body. How will I bear it? I CANNOT BEAR IT! What the hell have I done?

Before I am allowed to go to bed, I am given a sheet of paper to write down my thoughts from today. Words fail me. I have barely uttered a word since I arrived this morning. In horror, I begin to write of the fear that engulfs me. I explain that I have made a huge mistake in my decision to come here, that I am not like the others.

I am 39 years old, I am married with children, I have a career, a nice home, an income; everything I have spent my life trying to achieve, I have achieved. My life was the best polished veneer I had strived for years to create. But I had created a false sense of self, an acceptable presentation to others, because the truth wasn't acceptable. I wasn't acceptable. I did not want the world to know the truth. I had tried so hard to 'make it', to make me and everyone else safe.

Finally, I am allowed to crawl into bed. I hold myself still, as small as possible, so that I become invisible, unseen, and unheard, to stay safe. I escape from reality and drift into a half sleep. Memories from the past engulf me…

1974

My mum went to off to work and I went to our neighbour's house – my mum's best friend, Auntie Shirley. She lived with her husband,

3

Dave, and brother-in-law, Arthur. Today, my friend Tracey and I play two balls on the street as she is staying at Auntie Shirley's, too.

'Come in for your tea now,' Auntie Shirley calls.

I am hoping for her best chip butties and sugar sandwiches that she gave us sometimes as a treat. We all sit down, except Dave who always stayed in the other room. I always thought he was a bit weird. After tea, Arthur says, 'I've got some new LPs to play you today. Come upstairs with me.'

He says this every single time.

I squeeze my teeth together whilst clenching my jaw to hold back the vomit that threatens me. I look to the floor I see my shiny new blue shoes. 'Special shoes for a special girl.' I force myself to remember. I am special; I am the one who has been chosen. The kitchen table, all those sat around it fade out of existence. I am alone.

I can't do this any longer.

I try to cover up my retching from the sight and stench of him.

I am floating above the bed. I am free. I am disconnected from myself and his actions. I am for a short time totally removed from the reality that is my young life.

'Such a pretty girl,' he repeats over and over. 'This will be our secret.'

I am ugly. I am dirty. I am worthless. I am nine years old.

I wake up in a cold sweat, I look around in the dark. There is no comfort, no home, no belongings, no family, just a bed, a partition, and some drug addicts to share the night with.

16 December 2004

'Rachel, get out of bed, you're late for group therapy.' My counsellor had come to my room.

'I'm not getting up, I feel really ill, I'm so tired,' I said.

'Get up, Rachel, the bell has rung. Treatment is not optional. Get up, get to group, or pack your bags,' he repeated.

'I hate this place, it's pointless. You don't understand the pain I'm in. I hate myself. I am such a failure,' I cried.

I felt incredibly sorry for myself. I should be at home. I was so, so angry – with myself, with everyone else, with the world. Yet the suffocating weight of sadness within me threatened my very existence. After five days of detoxing and eight days of hell in primary treatment, I lay in my bed wanting to be anyone other than me. I was ashamed. I was humiliated. Where was their care and compassion? The demanding schedule from 7.30am to 10pm every single day, had me raging inside like a caged animal. I was raw.

I missed being able to destroy myself if I chose. I missed being able to escape. I missed alcohol. I didn't know what to do any more; everything I had done to this point to make it better had landed me here. I wondered if I could get home. Could I reinvent myself again – a 'successful Rachel'? If I tried again to cut back, I'd be ok – wouldn't I?

Alcohol had aided my escape from reality like nothing else; all my practice over the years of disconnecting myself from life had been made simple by that first mouthful. All of the hurt was wrapped up, soothed, and sent off into the night, leaving me with the sweet taste of freedom in a fantasy world where the damage had never been done.

How could I live without my anaesthetic? I didn't think I could face the accumulation of torment inside me. Could I do this, or would I die? Did I want to die? Should I leave now? How the hell had I let it come to this? A permanent loop of thoughts constantly sped through my craving, addled mind.

I had made my own decision to come here; I had researched different clinics and decided this was what I needed to do. I had just lost my job – the best job I'd ever had.

'Rachel, are you getting up or are you leaving?' My counsellor brought me back to the present moment.

I had to make a choice.

I wanted to live.

I got up.

17 December 2004

'Have you started writing your life story, Rachel?' my counsellor enquired.

I hadn't. It was a requirement for all clients in the community. Later that day, I took a deep breath and began.

I improvised from the story my family relayed about how my life began:

1965

In the early evening, within a Victorian terraced house, my family of five were thrown into panic. I was five months old and life-threateningly ill.

'She's bleeding, there's blood in her nappy!' my father shouted.

The ambulance took us to the hospital.

'What's wrong with her, Doctor?' asked my mother.

'We need to operate; your daughter has an intussusception in her intestines. The dead tissue has become gangrenous. If we don't operate now, she will not make it. The intestine will have to be cut out, it's rotten.'

The doctor returned after a long night for my parents.

The operation was successful. She's going to be ok; we have removed the damaged ileum and she will make a full recovery,' he said.

I paused while I thought about how my child's mind had interpreted this dramatic start to my life. I don't remember how or why, but I concluded that:

I never should have been born.

I was born rotten.

I was a mistake.

I was rotten from the inside-out.

I was unlovable.

I do not have permission to live.

Somehow, I felt I was so poisonous I nearly died. I didn't want to be me. I wanted to cut myself adrift from myself, life, and everyone in it. I was alone. I was nothing. I punished myself.

I put my pen down; the bell was ringing. It was 7pm, and time to listen to someone else's life story.

'I'd like my case, please, I am going home. I cannot stay here, I am not safe with these people.' I ran to the nurses' station with the familiar adrenaline of fear. I had hit a new level of terror.

'This is not a world I know!' The story I had just heard – of extreme violence, drugs, guns, and death – was not something I could cope with.

'I am just a normal person, with a normal life. I will be ok now; I can do this at home.'

'Of course, you can have your case, but sit down and tell us what's happened. You are safe here with us,' said one of the nurses.

I sat down.

I got my breath.

I talked.

I talked for two hours.

I talked about my crippling fear of life, my children, my work. We had a 'normal' chat over a cup of tea. I felt relieved. I suddenly saw that they were 'normal' people doing a fantastic job. I felt heard. I started to see that I didn't need to be so fearful. A sense of clarity came to me as I saw that I was utterly lost to a world I didn't understand. Despite all my efforts, despite everything I had overcome to this point, I was lost. I couldn't 'do' life properly. I had worked hard, got an education later in life, got a good job, but it seemed the harder I worked at it, the more painful it got. I had failed so miserably. I needed the help just as much as everyone else.

A small glimmer of hope appeared. I woke up the next morning with a new perspective. I saw my own situation and those of others with less denial or prejudice. I began to feel some belonging. I knew that if I wanted to recover, I had to face myself. I had to take responsibility.

25 December 2004

'It's snowing!' we all shrieked.

The 10-foot fresh tree, complete with presents, wafted pine scent through the lounge where natural decorations from the grounds adorned the huge fireplace. Juliette and I sat in the large Georgian windowsills looking out to the deer mooching around. It was literally a picture-perfect Dickensian Christmas scene, inside and out.

The bell rang. A Christmas feast served by the chefs.

We played board games.

I laughed more than I had in a very long time.

I cried for the child I had abandoned in me.

This past week I had completed the writing and reading of my life story, which included 'The Deal' – a significant dictator of my adult life:

1971

The drunken shouting sent me flying off my bed. My stomach churned so quickly, I thought I would be sick. It was happening again – my mum drunk, her temper flaring as the flashbacks of previous times sped through my mind. I was going to die. I stood with my back against my bedroom door, tightly hanging onto my teddy. 'Please, God, please let me live. I'm so frightened. Don't let me die. Please don't let me die.' My heart was racing, my legs so weak, I knew I couldn't hold the door. I didn't know what was going to happen, the situation was out of control. I cried without sound; I was desperate. My seven-year-old self prayed, 'Please, God, if you let me live, when I grow up, I will spend my life helping other people, I promise. I will do everything I can to relieve their pain.'

The chaos stopped. I climbed into bed and slept as I did often, without moving a muscle. The deal was done. I had called on God – a God I didn't know or was sure was real, but in my child's mind I knew I would never go back on my word. If I thought I mattered before that night, I was now clear, that my life would only be about helping others. I had survived, therefore, I had permission to exist but not to live for my own wellbeing.

I read the whole sorry story of my life to date out to the community. I detailed the damage that had been done to me, the creation of my false self, the damage I had in turn caused others and to those I loved the most – my children.

Opening a small present, I felt myself relax. I could stop pretending. I had shared the worst of me and I had survived. Relief flooded through me.

The treatment programme was only minimally interrupted for the festivities. The work continued. I have no idea how, but I kept going, getting up every morning, doing my chores. I had paid a large amount of money to come here, and here I was sweeping up cigarette butts from the balcony, sweating over the industrial dishwashers, talking about my feelings in group and individual therapy, for what seemed like every minute of the day and night.

I had shifted from a place of prejudice to a place of compassion for others and for myself. I engaged, whilst still keeping myself safe. I still wanted to isolate myself at times, but I was given little choice but to face up to my failings daily.

8th January 2005

My husband and two older children were coming to a family therapy session today. They were likely going to tell me exactly how I have hurt them. I felt sick.

I sat in the chair.

I listened while my children described their experience of me, detailing the pain I had caused them, ironically repeating the fear I felt as a child. The fact that I had hurt them in a similar way was sickening to me.

I sat in the chair.

'You didn't defend or try to justify your behaviour. The children needed to say that, and you needed to hear it. Well done, Rachel,' said my counsellor begrudgingly. It was small praise that I did not deserve.

It was decided by the counsellor and the family that it would be best for me not to return home. Instead, I should move on to what they termed 'a secondary treatment facility' for a further six months. I was not going home. I had thought this journey was coming to an end, but no. More reality. It had only just begun.

19 January 2005

The bell rang and continued to ring out for my leaving ceremony. The whole community came together, circled around the atrium, sharing their love and best wishes. For 42 days and 42 nights, I had got up, I had done what was asked. I completed my treatment. Today, I was leaving the home I had had for six weeks – the place I hated; the place I felt so unsafe but which had become my safe haven.

I had simultaneously been confronted, challenged, and supported by the whole staff team, my peers, and my family. The events of my childhood had led me to mistaken beliefs about myself, my parents, and the adults around me.

It turns out it wasn't anyone's fault. I had abandoned the child inside me at an early age, and worked hard to hide these 'truths' about myself by creating a 'false' persona. I had stuck to the deal; I had spent years working with disadvantaged vulnerable adults to relieve their trauma.

However, in creating 'Rachel', I destroyed myself and damaged others. With every layer of protection, I had become more and more lost. The cost had been too high for all of us.

I know I have found a deeper strength – a resilience that I ever knew I had – in this beautiful environment. I know that I arrived a victim of 'my life', but l was leaving as an adult.

I choose to live. I choose to recover. I am entering life sober; without pretence. My life is my responsibility.

A message to my younger self...

If I could go back in time and speak to my younger self, this is what I would want her to know.

I want to tell you how I am in awe of your resilience, the courage you had to face yourself, to have the worst of you held up squarely and unreservedly in front of you. You wanted to run, to hide, to escape, but you stayed. You faced your demons, and that is the hardest thing anyone will ever have to do – to look in the mirror at your damaged self. Thank you.

You innocently decided that you were rotten, damaged, and broken, from which you set out on a path of self-destruction. All the striving for better, all the suffering you thought was you, all the years of trying to find the answer, the thing that would fix you. The constant need to escape life and the pain it held for you. I feel like I abandoned you. I'm sorry. I tried so hard to make it right. I wish you could have seen who you truly are.

Fifteen years ago, you put yourself into your worst nightmare and not only survived but learned how you had created such destructive beliefs that it nearly killed you. You learned the hard way that qualifications, careers, houses, relationships, and other material possessions do not provide internal peace or happiness. You innocently believed that creating a false persona, being a therapist to others, would make you acceptable to others.

If I could go back in time, I would want you to know that this is the misunderstanding of how we think life works. It doesn't. Life works from the inside-out and not the outside-in. Your accumulated beliefs were merely a collection of repetitive thoughts. They did not define you. Our thoughts do not define any of us; they are not who we are. In believing them, you hurt yourself and those you loved.

By surviving everything you have been through, you now know that we all think so many things every second of every day. We feel regret, guilt, and shame about the past. We worry about the future: What will happen to me? Will I be ok? What if this happens or doesn't happen? But the past and future can only exist in our present-day thoughts about things. We have to think about the past in the present moment to bring it to life; we have to have thoughts about the future in the present moment to imagine it.

13

The experience you went through showed you how, when you really think about it, your thoughts created your reality that brought you to rehab in 2004. This process taught you that this type of thinking was the root of all your anxiety and depression.

You thought the pain of life would break you. It didn't.

You thought you would never be happy. You are.

You were never rotten, damaged, or broken. The problem was you thought you were.

I am the essence of life.

I am The Girl Who Refused to Quit.

Dedication

To my girls: You are my inspiration. Follow your own journeys with love.

About the Author

Rachel lives in a small village in Devon. She has been described as a 'compassionate, inspiring and powerful coach'.

When she's not coaching, running workshops or spending time with clients, Rachel can be found hanging out at home writing, reading, and taking time out for herself, alongside being with her family.

Rachel is beyond passionate about facilitating change in others, to free them from their own negative thoughts towards freedom.

Her mission is to share with other women a simple understanding that changed everything for her, by bringing hope, love, and inspiration to the conversation.

Contact

www.onewomansjourney.co.uk
rachel@onewomansjourney.co.uk
Facebook One Woman's Journey
Rachel will be publishing her first book, *One Woman's Journey,* in 2020.

Finally Finding My Voice

Kate Fernandez

ENOUGH!!! I am in charge of what you do to me, I want to know what's happening! My frustration reached boiling point as I ripped the feeding tube out of my nose. I couldn't take it any more. I couldn't speak or swallow, let alone scream out loud. But I also couldn't stop the rage that had been building inside me for far too long.

I had endured 22 hours of surgery over two days, only to find out a few days later that I had a blockage in my neck which required yet another operation. The third visit to surgery was a turning point in my life! I felt with every bone in my body that I was incredibly lucky to have survived that trip to theatre, but made a conscious decision that when I did finally come around from the anaesthetic, enough was enough.

My entire life had consisted of me not speaking up, never voicing my opinions, feeling like my voice didn't matter, or being very quickly silenced if what I was saying didn't want to be heard. Now, here I was, *literally*, with no voice. It was in that very moment that I knew something had to change. I remember the look of horror on the nurses' faces as they tried to calm me down and reinsert the tube.

They must have thought I had lost the plot. Despite being drugged up on copious amounts of pain relief and knowing that I had a long road of recovery, I also knew there were going to be some big changes in my life. It was time for me to finally find my voice.

It seemed crazy that only 12 weeks prior to the operation, I had been living a relatively 'normal' life. I had my fair share of good and bad times, but my old life (and face!) were now unrecognisable. I had no idea if either would ever be the same again, and that was extremely scary.

It all began back in April 2012 when I was unwell and diagnosed with shingles due to a very unpleasant rash around my neck and throat. I was given anti-viral medication by an out-of-hours GP. A couple of weeks after this, I developed a sore lump under my tongue. The shingles disappeared but the lump didn't. I booked an appointment with my own GP, who told me not to worry and that the lump would go away in a few weeks. But the pain in my mouth got increasingly worse.

I had a routine dentist appointment a week later, and I mentioned the horrendous discomfort to the hygienist. I was due to go on holiday in a few days, so they managed to get me seen that day by the dentist who was on duty. I was told to take antibiotics, rinse with mouthwash, and to enjoy my holiday. I booked an appointment for two weeks later with my own dentist, then took their advice and trusted that my sore and swollen tongue would soon be back to normal.

On my return from holiday, my own dentist examined me and immediately knew something wasn't right. I was referred to our local hospital, where I was booked in for, what I assumed to be, an initial consultation. Due to the increased pain and swelling, and the reduced movement of my tongue, the registrar was unable to carry out the examination herself.

Instead, she asked if I could wash my hands and attempt to lift up my tongue to show her the affected area. I will never forget the alarmed look on her face before she asked for me to be seen by another consultant downstairs. I was already feeling tired and weary after what had been a very long day of waiting, but made my way downstairs, innocently unaware that the worst was yet to come.

The pain that seared through my body as the nurse took the biopsies was almost unbearable! The memory still sends shudders through me now. I remember thinking that I would rather cut my own tongue off than repeat that vile procedure. I wiped the tears from my eyes, took a deep breath and composed myself before she repeated the procedure for the second, and then the third time!

A week later, rested and (just about!) recovered from the ordeal of the biopsies, I went back to the hospital for my results. I can't remember the exact words, but basically, I was diagnosed with a squamous cell carcinoma of the tongue – cancer of the tongue. I'll be honest, it didn't really come as a huge surprise. It did, however, come as a massive shock to my partner who had come with me to the appointment for moral support. I saw the colour drain from his face and he looked like he had been hit by a tank!

I was 44 years old, a mum to two gorgeous girls – aged 27 and 17 – a partner, a daughter, a sister, and a friend. In what felt like a blink of an eye, I was now also a cancer patient. Cancer of the tongue is normally associated with heavy drinkers and smokers, and in some cases HPV (Human Papillomavirus). In my case, I felt wholeheartedly that it was brought on by stress.

I had been going through a really tough time in my life, and had been under immense levels of stress. Only six weeks prior to my own cancer diagnosis, my mum had been diagnosed with breast cancer. I had been supporting her physically and emotionally whilst she recovered from a mastectomy in the same hospital where I now sat.

Everything happened so quickly. One minute I was being told of my diagnosis, the next I was being told about the huge and very risky operation that was to follow. I tried my hardest to absorb the fact that they would need to sever my tongue, taking enough away to completely remove the tumour. They would then need to do a skin graft from my left arm, which would include a nerve. This would then be used to reconnect my tongue and the nerves down my left arm, which would enable me to still use my left arm and, 'all being well', enable me to be able to learn to swallow and speak again!

The final part of the surgery jigsaw was where they would take flesh from my stomach to refill the area in my arm that had been removed. I can laugh about this part now, as I always refer to it as my added bonus of a tummy tuck!

When I was first diagnosed, I was carrying more weight than I would have liked. I tried to stay positive, but sadly there are many risks with this type of surgery, including learning to eat and swallow again. You initially lose weight with the worry and stress of the diagnosis, and then you physically struggle to eat for sometimes weeks or months. I was not able to have a Percutaneous Endoscopic Gastrostomy (PEG) feeding tube fitted, so it was decided that I would have a nasal gastric tube which would go up my nose and into my stomach to allow liquid feeds to keep me going.

From the ward where I was diagnosed, I walked in disbelief to the breast cancer ward, where I explained that I might need a bit more help supporting Mum as I had just received some devastating news of my own. They were amazingly supportive.

I remember going home that afternoon in a state of shock. I was scared for myself, but more for my family and how this would impact upon them.

I want to acknowledge the most amazing team who took care of me at Russells Hall and New Cross Hospitals. This includes surgeons, anaesthetists, an oncologist, a speech therapist, physiotherapist, radiographer, nutritionist, and the most amazing clinical nurse specialists and staff on the wards. It may sound like a strange thing to say, but I had to trust with all my heart that they would help me get through this whole experience, and I kept that thought every single day. I knew that I would be in the very safe hands of the experts, but unfortunately there was one part they couldn't help me with – the part I dreaded the most. Telling my daughters.

My youngest daughter was taking her A levels at the time that all of this was happening. I can vividly remember a meeting with my consultant at which he reiterated very strongly the need to tell family and close friends about my diagnosis. I would… as soon as I had a plan.

Following on from the diagnosis, I had CT and MRI

scans so that the surgeons could pinpoint the area of the tumour. The MRI experience was one I will never forget. I was looked after by a lovely gentleman who suggested I should imagine I was somewhere beautiful during the scan. I imagined that I was lying on a sun lounger on my favourite beach in the south of France! I got through the MRI and, if you can believe it, actually fell asleep!

The planning continued at the hospital, and I did eventually let the information out, but not until my youngest daughter had finished her last exam. One valuable piece of advice I had been given by my lead surgeon was to keep those who loved and would support me incredibly close, and not allow those who I felt would not support my decisions near me whilst I was going through the surgery and treatment. This may sound harsh, but it makes perfect sense – you need as much love and support as you can muster.

The time between diagnosis and surgery was spent writing my will, setting up a power of attorney for financial matters as well as for health and wellbeing. The health and wellbeing POA is your opportunity to plan who can act on your behalf if you are no longer able to communicate or make decisions for yourself. I took specialist legal advice on this.

So, the time came for my surgery, along with 17 days in hospital, with the possibility that I might not be able to speak again and might lose the use of my left arm!

I was admitted to hospital early in the morning the day before my surgery in June 2012.

Miraculously, I managed to sleep that night. The ward specialised in head and neck surgery, and the staff were incredibly kind and supportive even before the operation had taken place.

On the day of my surgery, I wrote in my notebook:

12th June 2012

6.25am – washed, gowned, and ready.

I have every faith in the team looking after me. They have explained what they plan to do, and I am positive that all will be well.

My thoughts, as ever, are with all my family and friends, but I know their thoughts are with me.

I am strong.

I woke up in recovery after 11 hours of complicated surgery. I was so frightened, and I couldn't speak! I had a tracheotomy, and looked like I had hit a brick wall at 250mph! I was surrounded by nurses who were checking wires and tubes and taking vital observations. I was incredibly scared, and wanted to communicate with more than just my eyes. My face was completely disfigured by the surgery, so facial expressions were useless at this point. Eventually, I got them to understand that I wanted a piece of paper and a pen so that I could communicate. They found a clipboard, paper, and pen, and I could then begin to express what I wanted. I was as high as a kite on morphine at this point and other drugs.

Unfortunately, this wasn't the first time I had been in a recovery room. I lost my husband 16 years ago to a Grade 4 brain tumour. He went through a massive operation.

There was the most amazing nurse in the recovery ward with my husband, and she asked me if I wanted to watch her take care of my husband or to help. I helped her that day, and that insight meant I understood so much more of what was happening to me in the recovery ward.

I couldn't use my left hand at all, as it was so heavily bandaged from that part of the surgery. But I felt relieved that I had survived this first round of surgery, and was transferred onto a ward.

My first night on the ward was one of many horrendous nights. There was an elderly lady across the ward who thought I was her daughter; she kept calling out to me, and asking the nurses why I wasn't speaking to her. I couldn't speak to anyone, no matter how much I wanted to! The following day, things weren't going according to plan. My new tongue was dying, and it was then that it came to light that the first operation hadn't worked and the nerve into my arm had not been connected. So, off I went, back into surgery the following day for a further 11 hours!

Everything initially progressed well until they found that I had a blockage in my neck. This resulted in my third major operation three days later. This led to my outburst of frustration, which led to ripping the tube out of my nose, which led to my decision that a change was going to come.

I understand that this was also a hard time for my family. My mum, cousin, partner, and daughters visited me in the first few days, and the sight must have been shocking. I can only imagine how awful those visits were. But I wanted to prove to each and every person that saw me that I was strong enough to get through this and that I would make a full recovery.

The days were filled with the all usual checks, and the nights were horrendous! I had one night where I listened continually to the album *Anthems,* by Russell Watson. I was so frightened that if I shut my eyes, I wouldn't wake up again. Russell Watson had survived a brain tumour and returned to his singing career. My thoughts were that if he could do it, so could I!

The power of music was also felt with another track, *Angels,* by Robbie Williams. (As I am writing this, I am listening to that song again.) I was surrounded by angels whilst I was in hospital, because that is the view I had of the most amazing team who took care of me. There were a few not so pleasant experiences, but I have learnt that holding onto those scary situations and the anger I felt only hurts me now.

I think this might be a good point to tell you about some of the personal insights I had whilst I was in hospital. I had an interest in complementary therapies after the death of my husband. After seeing all the trauma and pain he went through with surgery, chemotherapy, and radiotherapy, I wanted to find a gentler approach to life, so I decided to train as an Aromatherapist. This was fascinating, and I learned a lot.

However, what I hadn't bargained on was my reaction to treating male clients. I was happy to work on ladies, and passed all my assessments, but when I found myself in a treatment room with a man, I freaked. What I hadn't thought about for many, many years was the abuse that I had received as a child. All the fears and anguish just came flooding back. This meant my skills were confined to being used for myself, my daughters, and a few close friends.

A few years later, I continued my wellbeing journey and decided to become a Reiki practitioner. I enjoyed learning something that could help me be well and strong, and help my family, too.

This also helped in so many ways with my recovery from cancer. When I was lying in my hospital bed fighting for my life, I remembered that I had the Reiki symbols on my Kindle. So, I would lie in bed and draw the sacred symbols on my scars and wounds. The other thing I did that made the nurses look at me strangely was exercises moving my toes, feet, and ankles four times a day to keep the circulation going. I was having anti-coagulant injections, but I wanted to keep the blood flowing and I thought the exercises would help. I think they thought they had a nutter on the ward. They hadn't seen the half of it at this point!

My stay in hospital lasted 17 days, and my goodness I was pleased to be discharged. On that first day home, I wanted to sit and eat with my family, so this was planned. And I wanted a curry! Yes, that's right, I wanted something with flavour. Everyone enjoyed their food with texture and flavour; mine, however, had been pureed in a blender! Oh well! From that moment on, though, I became my own wellbeing project, and I managed myself with spreadsheets and started my own holistic ways to heal myself.

I recovered quite well from the surgery, but after a short period of time I started my radiotherapy treatment. This was to be undergone every day for six weeks, with the weekends off for good behaviour – only joking – you need the weekends to catch your breath and sleep.

The team at the Deansley Centre were amazing, too.

The scariest part was having to wear a mask made of a mesh which is moulded to the shape of your face. This is used each day to make sure that the radiotherapy therapy is hitting the correct spots – in my case, both sides of my neck and my tongue. The mask is also used to attach you to the radiotherapy bed! My first experience of this was horrendous, but I became more accepting of it and counted down the days to the end of my six-week treatment. A few years after my treatment had finished, I actually found my mask in the spare room. I took pleasure in stamping on it and throwing it away when I felt ready to let it go!

The radiotherapy is cumulative, and it keeps on working in your body well after the six weeks. My cousin had planned her wedding, which I was adamant I wanted to attend, on 21st September, 2012. My last two radiotherapy treatments were on the 31st August, and the hospital staff had some doubts about whether I would be well enough to go to the wedding. I had no doubts! I was going, even if that meant buying a big beautiful hat to cover up my scars.

After my surgery and during my treatment, I asked my partner if he would take me to London. We actually did this twice! We went to see *Mamma Mia,* and the closing ceremony of the Paralympics at Wembley! Coldplay were playing at Wembley, and I even found my squeaky voice to join in. It was incredible!

So, let's move on to the present day – October 2019! Over seven years have passed, and life has been good in places and tough in others. That's real life but I have learnt a lot. Yes, I experience some difficulties as a result of my surgery and treatment, and in some ways the mental scars are almost harder to heal than the physical ones which I see every day.

I have made some amazing memories since my illness, including walking my eldest daughter down the aisle on her wedding day, and attending my youngest daughter's graduation. I intend to be here to give my youngest daughter away, too – not that there is any rush!

A message to my younger self...

If I could go back in time and speak to my younger self, I would tell her with great love and honesty not to be so hard on herself.

As a caring person, you feel that it is necessary to put other people's needs and wishes before your own, but this doesn't need to be the case. Life is meant to be enjoyed, not endured – and this is key. Make the most amazing memories, and have the most amazing adventures, and share your love of life with your family and friends. That is what matters most.

I wished I had known how important it is to take care of yourself – simple things like getting your hair done, wearing beautiful bright clothes that make you feel special, confident, and comfortable in your own skin. Make sure you have plenty of time in the great outdoors. Nature will bring you peace and health.

Be more creative with your cooking, and let that creativity spread into other parts of your life, maybe painting and sewing. You may not paint a masterpiece, but that really doesn't matter. There will always be tough times in your life, but make the absolute most of the good times so you can keep on going.

Being able to survive everything I went through showed me how incredibly strong and determined you can be when you need to be.

It has taught me about my body and how to take care of it in a holistic way so I can be here to make more memories with my beautiful family and friends. I now feel more confident and also more accepting of myself.

If you are going through a similarly hard time right now, I think you need to know that you can overcome more than you think, and find an inner strength.

I am stronger and braver than I ever thought I could be, and I am looking forward to the next chapter of my life.

I am The Girl Who Refused to Quit.

Dedication

For my family and friends who have loved and supported me through the good times and the bad xxx

About the Author

Kate, who lives in Worcestershire, has been described as 'the kindest person I have ever known'.

When she's not carrying out her duties as a Trustee of The Healing Horse Sanctuary or immersing herself in her complementary therapies, Kate can be found supporting her family and friends or walking in the countryside. Kate has had an enlightening journey which has culminated in her becoming an aromatherapist, an Infinite Energy Healer and a Reiki Master. Kate's mission is to be a beacon of light to shine the way for others and inspire them to never quit.

Contact

kate@scattergoodtherapies.com
www.scattergoodtherapies.com
www.thehealinghorsesanctuary.org.uk
Kate will be publishing her first book, *Finally Finding My Voice*, in 2020.

Learning to Stay on Track
JoJo Ellen

August 2019

Tears streamed down my face as my head continued to spin. I felt absolutely lost. *Why does this keep on happening to me?* From the outside looking in, you may think I'm one of those girls who has her shit together – and to be honest, most of the time I do. But I was curled up in a ball on my sofa, under my blanket, crying my eyes out. I felt lost in my own head and lost in the world, without any direction. My head and my heart were having a battle. The crazy thing is that I knew what I wanted to do. I had huge goals and I know what I am capable of. I had been there before; I had done it all before!

So, why did I keep coming back to feeling this way? Had I just had enough of this line of work? Is it the people involved in this industry that's made me feel like this? Or is it my own limiting beliefs? Am I truly cut out for this world?

I felt as if my soul was just screaming and crying for help: help to be let out; help to get back on the path of least resistance!

I felt like every fibre of my being had been completely

damaged by the dog-eat-dog world I'd been a part of for so long. And it's so fucking hard to come back from it.

I remember when, six years ago, I first started working online within the network marketing industry. I was in love with the idea because it was different, and it seemed as if not too many people were doing it online back then. I didn't really seem to have the fears most people do when starting a business of this nature; I literally just went for it. Even though I had so many people doubting me, telling me it wouldn't work, and that I was just wasting my time, I felt compelled to give it my all – and I did.

But I soon realised along the way that the entrepreneurial journey is full of emotions! It's crazy, because the minute you take that plunge and decide you want to take this route in your life, it's like getting on a rollercoaster ride. It feels like you're standing on a ledge alone – just waiting for your turn, but never really having anyone behind you cheering you on. You sit in that rollercoaster cart and you're slowly going higher and higher up those tracks. Everyone around you is watching from the sidelines – waiting for you to change your mind; to 'see sense and give up'; or waiting for you to get so scared that you jump out of the cart and rush back to the safety of what's deemed 'normality'.

But you know that over that first drop, after you take that huge leap of faith, is a future that you so want to create and live by design, so you do it! You've jumped into the unknown, not knowing where this ride is going to take you.

One minute you're on an absolute high and feeling the intense vibration within your soul, breathing in every aspect of excitement you can feel; the next minute, you're feeling the lowest of the low, dropping deep into the abyss of depression and suicidal thoughts. Wondering if this is what you really set out to do.

It's crazy, because when you think about being an entrepreneur and having your own business, you don't think about the struggles, you don't think about the lows. All you think about is the success it brings, and the highs we feel, the income, the lifestyle.

I used to look at other successful people and think 'lucky them', but really, what I didn't think about is the journey they've had to go on, the people they've had to become to get where they are now. You just don't think about it! And I know that now, because I have had to go through those struggles to get where I am today!

I have learned a lot of lessons on my entrepreneurial rollercoaster. I have learned the hard way, I have struggled, I have felt immense pain, I've experienced the victim mindset and wanting to throw the towel in. But I have also hit huge milestones in my business, and I have succeeded far more than failed, and I have become a much better and stronger person for it!

Even though, I've always worked hard and done well, I've gone throughout my entire journey always feeling so misunderstood. And regardless of this feeling, I always strived to move forward, knowing what I wanted and where I wanted to get to. I always worked extremely hard and never gave up, because my dreams mattered.

The reason why I always felt so misunderstood is because I always struggled to fit in. Now, I don't know if again this was just my subconscious limiting belief, but I always felt as if no-one understood me and who I actually was as a network marketer, as an entrepreneur. I also thought deep down that because I am a very blunt character – I speak my mind and I don't follow the crowd – that maybe people just didn't like that. Then I thought: are people just jealous of the level of success I have had AND by doing things differently? I honestly couldn't tell you, because I'm not 100% sure, but all I know is that feeling had always been there and it's that feeling that's made my rollercoaster ride a hell of a bumpy one.

Last year, I started to lose my passion for the network marketing industry. I walked away and entered the world of coaching. I had always had a passion for mindfulness, personal development, and spirituality, and felt I was being pulled in a different direction. The rollercoaster changed direction and I started seeing so many heights I never thought possible. This was it! This was my true calling. The clients were flying in, my group programmes sold out, and my membership skyrocketed.

I was high on life and never wanted to get off! Time went on, and the online space became even busier and busier. So many people I knew from the network marketing industry were judging what I was doing; I was called names; I was slated on social media; and people really tried to bring me down.

I know that you need to tread carefully when dealing with people and social media, etc, and I know for a fact I have ruffled feathers and pissed people off because I've never held back, I know what I want and I'm not afraid to get it but at the same time, I have always said it is so important to be true to who you are and that you shouldn't have to 'watch what you say' just to get approval from certain people.

Have you ever felt worried about taking action or levelling up because you're worried what people are going to say about it?

Or perhaps your passion runs really deep and you have a voice within your soul that's trying to get out, but no-one is listening? This voice you know will impact so many people's lives, but no-one is taking you seriously.

Maybe you've made mistakes along your way; I certainly have! Gosh, when I first started out in this industry, I was a whiner! I was a gossiper. I was all about the drama, and I had a lot of run-ins with certain people. But I'm not being funny, who isn't like that when they're a naive 20-year-old and have had a life full of pain and suffering? Not to say others haven't, too, but hey, we all deal with situations differently, right?

Even though I had these experiences and felt the way I felt back then, I still had that inner feeling of 'but I'm still being true to myself'. I only ever live with pure intentions and I was struggling to understand why entrepreneurship was so difficult, how people out there can be so cold and try to dim your shine, how difficult it felt to get your voice to be heard, your message to be seen. The problem was that I was letting all of that get the better of me.

I know that it takes serious determination and hard work to break through to success. It's been really hard work getting to this point, I'll be honest. I've had so many times where I've worked so consistently hard in my business, putting in 12-hour days, not sleeping great, skipping meals, just so I could get work done. The hustle was real! I started resenting my business, because I was earning money on paper but not living the lavish lifestyle that's supposed to come with being an entrepreneur! But I soon came to realise is that it's not just about the action you take, it's the person you are when taking this action, and it's releasing the bullshit within your own mind to help you to progress. This is something I have had to master in all my years of working online and being self-employed. It certainly is a rollercoaster of emotions! So many highs and, sometimes, what feels like even more lows.

It really is tough being an online entrepreneur at times. The online space is so noisy; there's so much judgement and criticism and negative opinions!

Let me see if you relate to this. You know you're good at what you do, and you have a huge voice within your soul that's just ready to be set free and be heard! But sometimes, you develop imposter syndrome; sometimes you fall off the rollercoaster and find yourself on another track that's leading you even further down to the abyss of negative self-talk and self-doubt.

I know how hard it is to get yourself back up and to keep going. It's one thing carrying on, when you're working every waking hour to keep your business going, but then it's a whole other kettle of fish when opinions and other people come into it.

I remember at the start of my journey I had so many people telling me I was foolish, that I should go and get a real job, and I would never do well from it. That took me a long time to get over.

Can you relate to that? How many times did people tell you to just go get a 'normal' job? I always used to think to myself: 'well, what's even normal?'

This was a battle I had for the first few years of my

career, but I soon got over it because the money started rolling in. Isn't it funny, though, you start 'making' it and earning a good wage, yet you still feel so unaccomplished or like you have so much more of a way to go! You still feel you're being judged, or that no-one is taking you seriously. I've literally had it my entire journey of this career path!

Have you ever felt like there's a little voice within your head, or the naughty devil on your shoulder telling you negative self-talk? 'No-one will join your team.' 'No-one will buy your programme.' 'You aren't as good as her.' 'Your content isn't as professional or authentic.' I have literally heard it all, but from myself!

I mentioned earlier how I was judged when I first started working online. Well, I have actually been judged the whole way through, and still am now. But the funny thing is, it's not just people that I know that don't believe in what I do. It's people who do the same things I do! And it's stuff like this that caused me to self-doubt!

It's been so hard to not let other people's opinions get the better of me, and it's really difficult not to take on board what people say about you, too.

What I've found really difficult to deal with is when people judge you for what you decide to do, when they always have something to say about a programme you choose to create, or changing your company when you're in network marketing. Someone always has something to say! And I finally got to a point in my life, crying under my blanket on that sofa, thinking, *I am so sick of the world we live in. I am so sick of the way people treat other people. I am so tired and fed up of working so much and being stuck inside my business!* I was so sick of the nasty words people say about others

– the bullying online, the name-calling, and the judging! I was curled up in a ball that day because I literally felt as if that rollercoaster ride I had been on for six years, the constant highs and the continuous lows, had just come to a complete crash! Over. Finito!

It was because of how much negativity I had experienced, and things I'd seen written about me on social media – that weren't even true! Emotions I'd felt, and things I had witnessed my good friends in the industry also go through; I'd had enough, and I was going to quit. I literally felt as if my time here had ended and it was time to try my hand at something else. I was ready to go back to all of those naysayers that ever doubted what I did and say, 'You know what? You were right to doubt me. Here I am, going back to a normal job!'

And I seriously thought for a while, what am I good at? I was bullied all throughout my school years, so a decent paid job was off the table because good grades didn't exist in my book as I never finished school properly. I was an outcast in my college years, even though I studied numerous courses and always came out with the best grades. I never found my fit with anyone or anything as, again, I've always been different, and misunderstood, and never progressed because there was no passion for those career paths. I had no idea what kind of job I could do, because the only passion I had was for what I had been doing the past six years.

So, that was it then. I was just scared, emotional, and almost having a 'not so' midlife crisis at the age of 27! I just had absolutely no idea.

Was I over-thinking? Was I being a complete drama

queen and over-worrying? Quite possibly, but this is what the entrepreneurial journey was doing to me.

Shortly after this event in my life, I went on holiday with my two best friends, Matthew and Amber. On the way there, I kind of explained to them what had gone on and how I had been feeling, and I just remember them saying, 'Come on, we're going on holiday! Let's just concentrate on having the best time.' I'll admit, I was extremely excited because it was the most needed break I had taken in a very long time AND it had come at the perfect time. However, I still couldn't get the negative emotions out of my system.

The whole week we were away, I had a wonderful time, and it was so special to spend it with two of the closest and most special people to me. But, again, I experienced negative thoughts, getting upset and emotional. The fear of losing everything and not knowing my direction in life kicked in, and I started to really over-think about what was next for me.

I remember us going to the beach, and I have the worst fear of the sea! I am a really strong-minded person most of the time, with a lot of determination, but when it comes to the sea, I am an absolute mess! The water was beautiful. It was clear blue, the sand was gorgeous, and I thought to myself, *I've got to do this. You've been through worse, Jo. If you don't like it, you can always walk in slowly, so you progress. One step at a time.*

Amber reached out her hand and said to me, 'Come on, you've got this. I'll hold your hand and we will do it together.' And it's funny, because my entire life, I've only ever done things by myself. I've supported myself my entire adult life. I've had to pick up the pieces when the shit hit the fan, so having someone so close to me say those words meant more than anyone will ever know.

And the most amazing thing happened. I had a breakthrough. Leaning on someone who I trust and who I know has my back through anything, I was able to beat my fear. And there I was underwater, swimming, with my full body under the sea – and I loved every single minute!

Something strange happened that day, and it's almost as if I felt a sudden switch in my mind; a complete energy shift. I felt different – but in a good way. I felt as if that was one of those moments where 'everything happens for a reason'. I felt as if I had been guided and it was the Universe's way of showing me that every fear can be conquered. As long as you have the right support, and you trust in the process, even if you go at things slowly, it's possible to overcome.

I thank my wonderful best buds for that day on the beach. They helped me to see that every problem is solvable, every challenge can be faced, and no matter how big or how small the fear is, if you push yourself you can do it.

Being under the blanket that day was one of the toughest moments in my life to date. I am usually a really resilient person; I've been hurt a lot, and I've supported myself from a very young age. My parents brought me up to work hard and to just keep on going, and that's exactly what I have done ever since.

I'm not the same person who I was a few months ago under that blanket. I have found a new power from within my soul. I've been knocked down so many times, but I have always got back up. This time is no different, other than I now have more fire, more passion, and more determination than ever before to achieve all of my goals!

A message to my younger self...

If I could go back in time and speak to my younger self, I would tell her to always keep in mind your goals. They mean something; they are important and should be valued.

I have learnt that no-one is perfect! Yes, I've made mistakes; yes, I've gossiped; yes, I've done things perhaps that I shouldn't have, or not handled things in a professional way at times. But guess what? Let's be honest here, most of the human race have done all of the above! Every single person has to learn for themselves. They have to embark on their own journey to get to their desired destination.

The challenges you face, the lessons you learn, and the obstacles you come up against, happen constantly, right? But remember, it's the person you become after those things happen. What's important is the way you look at the situation, how you deal with it, and how you pull yourself through it.

No matter how stuck you feel within your business or within a situation right now, it always starts with you and your mind. Without your mind being strong and in the right place, you will keep struggling, and you will remain subconsciously blocked from ever moving forward or manifesting the results you want within your life and your business.

If you're feeling stuck right now – Stop. Take a huge step back. Go and take a day to completely switch off, do something that lights up your soul and remember your why. Come back with a fresh head.

The workload will get easier; remember you're doing

this for a reason. Just keep going. People will judge you, have an opinion, and continue to try and bring you down whatever you do. But realise this: whatever happens, trust that everything is never a reflection of who you are – it's a reflection of who they are. It just shows that they still have a way to go on their inner growth journey. All you can do is wish them well and give them gratitude for being part of yours. Give them thanks for giving you the fire and the determination to keep going. Spoiler Alert: The more success you get, the harder it gets, girl!

So, never let anyone take your power. Get back on the rollercoaster, stay on the tracks, enjoy the highs, and embrace the lows, and remember to have fun! It's all part of the journey.

And hey! Every struggle is worth it – it helps us to grow and become stronger, better people.

So, ask yourself this now: all those opinions of other people, the names, the bullying, and the doubts which cause you to not be your best self and do things that light you up inside – are they worth it? Is it worth quitting your true passion? No, it's not! Because your dreams matter, and somebody's opinion of you shouldn't have the ability to be able to steal your power and take away what means the most to you.

I will never let *anyone* take my power away again. I will always keep going.

I am strong, I am determined, and I am meant for more in this life.

I am The Girl Who Refused to Quit.

Dedication

For every single person who has ever been misunderstood in business, mistreated, and felt like they didn't belong. You've got this!

About the Author

Jojo, who lives in Bedford, UK, has been described as a spiritual coach who serves from the heart and soul.

When she's not mentoring her academy members and clients, she is travelling the world or enjoying a nice prosecco with her partner.

She's extremely intuitive, follows her heart, and is committed to her spiritual growth journey.

Jojo is very passionate about helping others to heal from within. It's her mission to ensure she impacts the world with her story, and shows people that no matter what you go through, you truly can have it all if you trust, keep working on yourself, and never let anyone get you down.

Contact

Femalepreneursacademy@gmail.com
www.femalepreneursacademy.com
Facebook/JoJoxEllen
Instagram/jojo_ellenx

The Seven-Year Itch

Emmalina Rebecca

What the F**k have I done! Standing alone in the middle
of a cold basement flat with a few belongings at my feet, I
looked down to see my former life packed into five basic
black bin liners. I had nothing to show for the last seven
years of my life other than these meaningless clothes. Had
I made a mistake? I stood in shock, not knowing what to
think as I continued to stare into space.

Silence was all around me and yet my thoughts were
deafening. They continued to consume me as I felt
incredibly overwhelmed, alone, and guilty. Guilty that it
was me who had decided to make this decision. Maybe I
should have just stayed?

I plonked myself down on one of the bin liners and
listened to the air squeezing out as I let out a huge sigh
and burst into tears! How had my life come to this? It was
December 2011, and I had just made the most painful
decision of my life to end a seven-year relationship and
start out on my own.

My tears fell uncontrollably as my head continued to
spin. How did I even have a right to cry? I was the one
who had ended it; I was the one who had put myself in this

position; so why should I be allowed to feel upset? Would it be too late for us to try again? It had been a wonderful relationship for the most part. It had its ups and downs, like most relationships do, so why would I choose to do this to us? Deep down I knew, though, I didn't want to go back.

I felt like such a failure, as a girlfriend and at life in general. I never felt good enough, always as though I was trying so hard but never really getting anywhere. What was I doing wrong? Things were not supposed to be this way.

Other women my age were settling down, getting engaged, having children. And here I was, at 26 years of age, sitting on a bloody bin bag feeling utterly shit about life. When I was little, I would always say, 'When I'm 25, I will get married and have children.' That was a definite. That was just the plan. It was concrete, and I would be so excited of visioning that goal as a young girl. Well, that didn't go to plan, did it? I didn't know what the bloody plan was now; I guess I was on a no-plan plan. FFS!!!

My tears ran dry and I sat once again in silence. 'Get a grip, Em,' I told myself. I'd never grieved over a relationship, but all I wanted was for my ex-boyfriend to be happy. He would say that he wasn't happy with anything in life, so I genuinely thought that if I removed myself from his life, he'd have one less thing to be unhappy about.

I felt that I was always trying to make others happy, always thinking about their needs and what they wanted. I always felt guilty about something, although I never really knew why. What I did know was that I was fed up of feeling guilty; I wanted to get over this shit. What did I even have to feel guilty about? This was my life and I deserved to live it on my terms!

The main reason I had decided to end my relationship was because I was feeling this urge, a need, a knowing, to soul search and find true happiness. I wanted this so bad. It had become a constant distraction in my life and I could never just sit and relax. Each time I did, my mind would continue racing with this need that I kept feeling. It started at my feet, swirled around heavily in my tummy, before rising to my heart, and finally sitting heavily in my mind.

Have you ever thought that what other people see of your life isn't entirely the reality of it? I felt like I was looking at my life as a beautiful carousel that you would see at the fairground. They are so mesmerising to look at, so peaceful, full of pretty colours as they represent a wonderful fairytale. However, I felt I was just going around and around and around. And I felt like screaming because I wanted it to stop. I wanted to get off and wander in a different direction.

What the hell was I was even searching for? What direction was I even wanting to go in? It was just this constant damn feeling screaming inside of me to DO IT! Do what? And why? Why the hell was I feeling this way, thinking this way?

Upon really reflecting, I knew there was another reason. My mum. Most days after work and each weekend, I would visit and see her so poorly, often confined to her bed. I would think how Mum would give anything to be able to have a decent quality of life and not be in endless pain. So, if my mum can't have this, then I refuse to waste my life not being happy when she provided me with this beautiful gift of me being here on Earth. I needed to go and find happiness. I needed to show her that her youngest child could have all the things that she had always wanted for me. I wanted to make that change and go out into the world independently, and grab opportunities and happiness with both hands!

It was a contributing factor, but it wasn't the only reason. My previous relationship to this one had been utterly horrendous, one that I could write a book on in itself! I walked out on that one without an ounce of guilt or regret, and I never looked back. So, maybe that's why I felt a complete disconnection with myself for the way I was feeling before I made the decision to walk away from this relationship.

Wow! I had been sitting on the same black bin liner in the middle of the floor for over two hours! Sitting in silence, with nothing but my own thoughts and a bottle of wine which I had now, without even realising, finished. I really should begin unpacking; after all, this was my new home! Urgh, I was tired. I needed another drink. I wondered if the shower was powerful; I would like a nice hot shower.

My thoughts would not stop, my mind would not rest. I was still trying to rationalise the decision I had made. Was I a bad person? Perhaps I didn't deserve the good things in life? Maybe this was karma because I had been a handful as teenager? Maybe this was payback for the underage drinking and smoking? Hang on a second. I might have been a bit of a difficult teenager, but what the hell did any of that have to do with ME deciding to leave?

Aaaargh! Enough! Just STOP IT! Think about the actual reality of the here and now, Emma!

I'd gone from living in a beautiful three-storey townhouse to a dingy basement flat in a shared house, with eight total strangers living in the flats above me. The thought made me feel sick to my stomach; I'd never lived on my own before!

Perhaps what was even worse was that I was financially broke! I had a secret shopping addiction. I'd racked up thousands of pounds worth of debt, and had my head well and truly buried in the sand. I could often slip into depression – and each time I did, I would shop.

Mental health and wellbeing weren't really talked about at that moment in my adult life, and quite often I would hear other people judging those who had expressed they felt depressed. It kind of had a stigma attached to it. 'Well, they look just fine to me,' I'd hear others say as they talked about that person who had tried to call out for help and express how they felt. Therefore, I didn't choose to talk about my true feelings, and shopping would be the answer to help lift my mind from that dark place.

I would hide the clothes in my wardrobe and not even remove the tags half the time, because I knew I wouldn't actually wear them! The times I did decide to wear them, my ex would ask if the item was new and I would blatantly lie, saying I'd had it for ages. The red letters would come pouring in and I would hide them, too. Credit card companies would call me chasing payments, and I would feel sick listening to the voicemails, then resort to denial and delete them without returning the call. I'd become trapped in a cycle of shame. I had no idea how I would cope financially, and this terrified me. I wanted to go out and shop to make myself feel better, but like all the many, many times before, it only left me feeling empty and even more guilty.

This was going to be a new start; a new chapter in my life. I wanted to prove to myself and others that I could do this on my own. I was strong, I was independent, and I didn't need to be with anyone else to prove it. A friend said to me before I moved out that I was making a huge mistake and that I wouldn't be able to cope on my own. They had big reservations about the decision I was making, and they believed I wouldn't be able to cope financially either!

One thing I will never allow is someone telling me I can't do something because they have little faith in me. I will never ever accept this. The only person who has the damn right to tell me whether I can or can't do something is ME! This wasn't the only time I had been told that I wasn't capable or able to do something. It had happened numerous times in my life, and each time I had always worked my absolute hardest to prove to them. 'I can, and I will.'

This time would be no different. I would prove to anyone who doubted me standing on my own two feet, living on my own, and providing for myself, that they were wrong. Done with all the thinking (and the wine!), I ended my thoughts on that positive note, jumped in the shower, made the bed up, clambered in and fell fast asleep. Tomorrow would be a new day. I would find a way.

The next day, my dear big brother Paul came to visit. He helped me give the place a really deep clean and unpack, then ordered a takeaway for us whilst we sat and chilled listening to music. I felt so much calmer and clearer, so much more level-headed. I knew I had made the right choice, and Paul reminded me that I always had our family and that they were all proud of me for following my heart.

My sister Kelly also popped round with my niece Lauren and nephew Ryan. They had a gift for me – some goldfish to keep me company! I'd never had fish before, but I was elated. One was orange, which I named Noel, and the other was yellow, which I named Liam, as I had always been a huge fan of the band Oasis. I don't think the Gallagher brothers would be too impressed that I named my goldfish after them, but it definitely made us all laugh.

It would have been great if Mum could have come for a visit, and I think I would have felt more settled if she had been able to visit. But she was still too unwell to get out of the house. However, Paul and Kelly reassured her that I was just fine. And do you know what? I did feel fine! All those deafening and consuming thoughts had finally gone!

I think it's the little things in life that count. Like being able to come and go as you please, being able to do what you want and how you want without feeling guilty. I was beginning to enjoy the fact that I didn't feel as guilty for things – possibly things I should never have felt guilty about. Like going to the gym for as long as I wanted to; lounging around, not having to do a great deal; not having to have tea ready every night, or the food shopping done. It was nice to just be me, to have a no-plan plan, when it seemed there had always had to be a grand plan.

The only plan I needed now was to sort out my finances once and for all, and to face up to the debt I had gotten myself into. It was time to put on my big girl pants and deal with this shit head-on. My sister was a fabulous help in this. We wrote down all my debts and she encouraged me not to hide any, as in doing so I was only hiding the reality from myself. I looked at the total figure written down and immediately burst into tears! I was so angry with myself. How had I let this happen? I felt utter shame, and the anger burned deep within me. I wanted to go into a field and just scream until there was no air left in my lungs.

What a disappointment I was! The things I could've spent that money on and had something to look back on and feel proud of. I could have saved it. But I might as well have just opened the toilet and flushed the whole amount of cash down it. I felt ashamed and, in some way, I actually felt sorry for myself. I was sorry for not doing something about it sooner, sorry that my only escape to my depression had been to shop. There was no point living with the regret now, though. I didn't need to make myself feel any worse about myself than I already did. If anything, it was the wake-up call I needed. I made a promise to myself that I would never deal with things in that way again. To this day, I never have – and that is something I feel proud of.

I made an appointment with Citizens Advice. An agreement was put in place to pay off all my creditors, and I worked out my finances to realistically see how much I would have left as disposable income each month. Let me tell you, it was crap. But I knew there would be so many other people far worse off than me! Christmas was approaching, and I was feeling drained and run down. Mum was getting worse, and it was painful to see her in this way.

I popped in to visit my sister on the way home from work, and she told me that she had been to visit Mum and she really wasn't so good. I hadn't seen Mum now for three days. Usually, if she was feeling unwell, she would text me to say not to visit as she didn't want me to get upset.

Although I would rather visit regardless, I honoured her wishes only because I didn't want her to feel she needed to put a brave face on for me. She didn't have to, but I felt a lot of the time she did. I made the decision to visit her the next day regardless of how she was, as I wanted to give her a big cuddle.

Driving home, I was in a world of my own, thinking about Mum, thinking about Christmas, thinking about finances, and about how much my life had changed in just a few months. I approached a crossroads and was going straight ahead. When a car flashed me out, I presumed there was no oncoming traffic so I proceeded to drive straight on. Unbeknown to me, there was a car driving down the main road to my left, which I hadn't seen for the queuing traffic, and I ploughed straight into the side of it, causing them to hit a cyclist, who flipped up over their car and onto the bonnet of mine!

The noise was deafening as I smacked my face into the steering wheel. Everything went blank. It felt like I had been sitting with my head on the steering wheel for an eternity. I came to and began screaming. WTF just happened! SHIT! I clambered out of the car and burst into hysterical tears, trying to make my way across the busy road to the car and the cyclist. I needed to know that they were ok.

Luckily, the driver, passenger, and cyclist were not too injured. I cried, desperately telling them how sorry I was. I was shaking so badly and could hardly breathe. The lady who was the passenger put her arms around me and told me it was ok. No-one was seriously injured, and she sympathised that it had just been an accident.

She asked if there was anyone I could call, but in that moment I felt so alone. I just wanted my mum! I didn't want to panic my brother, so I did what we all tend to do in a crisis – called my sister.

After the police had taken all the details, my sister drove me back to her house (my car was still driveable) where I stayed the night. I felt so blessed that I had a wonderful family and that everyone involved in the accident was safe.

It felt like everything had happened all at once. My life was at a crossroads, then the accident had been at a crossroads. I reflected on the break-up, the shit reality of my finances, the accident, and Mum gradually becoming increasingly unwell.

I still felt proud of the decision I had made to leave and venture out on my own. A new year was approaching, and I told myself that things couldn't possibly get any worse. It would be a totally fresh new start.

But what I thought had been a very dark time for me at the end of 2011 would be absolutely NOTHING in comparison as to what was around the corner!

A message to my younger self...

If I could go back in time and speak to my younger self, this is what I'd want to tell her.

You may feel right now that you are at a loss with yourself. You feel you are being pulled in a whole new direction without a plan. You may be scared to end your relationship because it provides the security of what you feel you need. This relationship may have served its purpose, and has taught you many great things to now go ahead in life with an understanding of what you do and do not want from a relationship.

I wish when I was feeling total overwhelm, fear, and confusion about ending my relationship, that someone could've told me that everything would be ok and to trust my instincts and truly believe in myself.

Being able to survive ending a long-term relationship and venturing out on my own taught me that I was much stronger as a woman than I knew. It was me who truly held the power within me to fulfil my own desires.

It has shown me that in making that huge step, I didn't need to crave for anything; I didn't need to buy material things to teach me how to love myself. It taught me how to become financially independent, to love and respect what I earned, and how to stand on my own two feet without creating financial difficulty. In following my heart, even though it felt scary, I truly learned to love myself, grow independently on my own, and be comfortable with my own company. This has led me to find my perfect soul mate and have the relationship I always longed for.

I now feel complete. My heart is full of love and joy, not only for who I am but for the person I became in making that huge leap of faith and trusting myself. I feel so much in love, and feel so blessed for the partner I have and for my beautiful stepdaughter. My life is complete, and I couldn't be happier.

If you are going through something similar right now, my advice would be to take that leap of faith. Do not burden yourself with the what ifs and what nots; do not worry about the material things you may have right now, if you are looking at it all and feeling empty.

Take that leap of faith and trust yourself. This is your life and your life alone, regardless of your circumstances. You deserve the right to true happiness. Believe in yourself, have your own back, and the Universe will have it, too. Your desires will be granted and much more, if only you take that first leap. You will not look back with regret, but you will live to be truly proud of the decisions you made and just how far you will go. We each have just one lifetime on this beautiful earth; live it with love and joy in your heart, and live it for YOU.

I am now a fiancée to my wonderful soulmate, I am a book author, and I have my own business, which wouldn't have been possible if I hadn't made that decision all those years ago, if I had just settled for what was.

I am blessed, and I am grateful for my life now.

I am damn proud of who I am. I am proud of how I followed my heart and trusted myself that everything would be ok.

I am The Girl Who Refused to Quit.

Dedication

For Johny Mccluskey, my soul mate x

About the Author

Emmalina Rebecca lives on the Fylde Coast of England, and has been described as an inspiration of hope and strength to others.

Alongside working full time, she runs her business, Little Lights of Attraction, making beautiful, spiritual, hand-made, hand-poured soy wax candles and melts.

When not working, Emmalina can be found relaxing with her soulmate, her fiancé, as well as teaching her adorable stepdaughter all about angels and crystals.

Emmalina's mission is to bring a light to others in the world and to help them to find the strength to never give up in life, no matter how painful it can be.

Contact

Facebook page: emmalinarebecca
Facebook group: Little Lights of Attraction
Emmalina Rebecca will be publishing her first book in 2020.

Light After Dark

Vimi Seewooruthun

with Cassandra Farren

This can't be happening! I walked silently into the hospital ward as I stared across the room in complete disbelief. My husband lay still, completely motionless, on his bed. A doctor stood over him, frantically pumping his heart. The bed was surrounded by a team of at least ten medics, but nobody saw or heard me. My breath quickened and my head began to spin. *What's going on? Why isn't he waking up?* I couldn't take it in. Everything was happening so quickly, but I was watching the nightmare unfold in slow motion. The machines bleeped frantically, the doctor continued to pump as my mind replayed what had happened only 10 minutes earlier…

I had received a phone call to say that my husband's condition had deteriorated. The nurse sounded serious, but calm, when she asked me to come in as quickly as I could. I still remember her words. 'Could you come in, please, your husband has taken a turn for the worse.' I asked what she meant, and if he was ok, but she replied, 'Please come in as soon as you can.' I remember thinking, *Oh he must have had a heart attack, but that would be 'ok', we can deal with that.* We would get through it together; we always got through everything together. I quickly dressed and made the very short journey to the hospital, trying to stay positive but not knowing what to expect. He had been in hospital several times with his condition and we knew he wasn't well, but he would receive the treatment he needed and then he would been okay. That was how it usually went.

It wasn't until I walked into the entrance of the hospital that an awful feeling of dread engulfed me. I quickened my pace and began running up the stairs to his ward. Then suddenly, I stopped. *What if something terrible was happening to him? What if I walked in and I couldn't cope?* I would have to deal with it on my own. I gave myself a quick talking to and reminded myself that we were only young. I was 33 and he was 34. We had only been married for one year and had the rest of our lives to look forward to. He was going to be okay. He *had* to be okay. There was still so much we wanted to do, there were still so many more memories to make.

I took a deep breath but couldn't shake off the fear that something didn't feel right. I tried to remain calm, but I didn't know what to do. *Should I run? Should I walk?* I wanted so desperately to be with him. But maybe, instinctively, I knew there was a chance I could lose him. I couldn't lose him. He was going to be okay. He would never leave me. I started to run until I arrived at the ward feeling out of breath and in complete shock at the heart-wrenching scene that greeted me.

The relentless noise from the machines brought me back to reality. I knew I must be awake, but my body didn't feel like my own. I watched in disbelief as the doctor continued to massage my husband's heart. My own heart pounded loudly as I silently prayed, willing him with all my might to wake up. Inside my head I was shouting, 'Come on, wake up. You've got to wake up, you're going to be okay!'

My legs started to feel weak then my thoughts were suddenly interrupted. I heard the words, 'Come with me' as I felt the arm of a nurse scooping around my waist. I was ushered into the hospital day room where my head continued to spin as I frantically paced up and down, repeating the same panicked questions over and over: 'What is happening now? How long is this going to take? When can I see my him?' All I wanted was for someone to come and tell me that he was okay. I was aware of the nurse being there, but I couldn't take in anything she said. I kept on saying to her, 'He's going to be alright, isn't he?' I think deep down she knew, but I continued to pace the room in shock, praying for a miracle. Everything went into slow motion, and every minute felt like an hour.

It was 30 long minutes later when the doctor finally walked in. I could tell by the look on his face that it wasn't good news, but nothing could have prepared for me for the soul-destroying words that followed. 'I'm so sorry,' he said, 'He didn't make it.' NO! The grief hit me like a tonne of bricks as my legs collapsed beneath me. I dropped to the floor crying inconsolably, hitting the radiator behind me as I fell. I held my head in my hands and rocked as the floods of tears streamed down my face. All I could think was what was I going to do. *I've got my whole life ahead of me, what am I going to do without him?*

The nurse tried her best to console me and gave me

some time before saying that I needed to call someone. Call someone? It dawned on me then that I was all alone. My brain couldn't think straight or function properly. *Who would I call?* I didn't know if I could stand up let alone speak, but she helped me up and agreed to call my younger brother. It was another long half an hour before he walked into the day room with his wife and found me shaking and still in shock. I looked at him and slowly shook my head as the tears began to stream down my face again. 'He's left me,' were the only words I could find. My brother picked me up and held me close in his arms, and I closed my eyes not wanting to see the reality I now faced. I couldn't believe he was gone. It didn't seem real.

A nurse came in to tell us that my husband's body had now been moved to another room, and she asked if we wanted to spend some time with him. I nodded and stood up, still in a daze. I wanted to see him, but I had no idea what to expect.

She led us into a big bright room; there was just a window, a bed, and a chair. Everything looked so simple, almost like it was out of a film set. I slowly walked over to where his body lay under a white sheet. I perched on the side of the bed and gently held his hand, surprised that it still felt warm. I had thought his body would have felt cold. *If his blood was still warm, maybe there was a chance that he could still wake up?* It just looked like he was sleeping; so peaceful and so calm. I wished so hard that he would open his eyes, that this was maybe all a bad dream? It would be a miracle, but there had to be a chance. In my mind, I pleaded, *Please, please wake up*. But he didn't move.

Everything was so still. But in that moment, a beautiful

beam of sunlight shone through the window and down onto his face. Wow! *Was this a sign?* My tears stopped. I was still in shock, but a feeling of peace began to wash over me. I reached out and gently stroked his forehead and his hair. 'You're not in pain any more,' I whispered. 'You're going to help a lot of people from where you are now. You can be a proper superhero.'

It felt so surreal that just a few days earlier we had been having a conversation about one of his favourite topics, superheroes. We had arrived at the hospital, waiting to be admitted onto a ward. I knew he was in a lot of pain, but I wanted to keep him positive. He'd spent his life living in pain, but despite this he always had the desire to help other people; he wanted to make a difference. As we sat in the waiting room, we'd spoken about planning a charity event to raise money once he got out of the hospital. As he was such a big superhero fan, we decided that this would be the perfect theme for our event.

He'd be gutted that he now wouldn't be able to attend his party (in human form), but it brought me some comfort to think that he could be his own superhero now. He could help more people all in one go from where he was now.

As the time passed, both my and my husband's close family arrived, along with his two best friends. I looked up to see his mate standing in the doorway, and quietly said to my husband, 'Your friends are here now.' I told him and his wife that it was ok, and that they could come over if they wanted to. I don't remember the words they said to me, but I remember looking into their big sad eyes. I continued to hold my husband's hand as I softly touched his wedding ring. 'It's going to be okay. It's going to be fine. You're going to be alright now. You're going to have lots of fun. Don't worry about us,' I assured him. 'Everything's going to be okay.' Maybe, deep down I was trying to reassure myself that *I* would be okay? It still didn't feel real that he'd gone. I knew it hadn't hit me.

I sat by his side for hours and didn't want to leave. It was getting late when my dad told me that it was time to go home now. *Go home?* I didn't want to go home. I felt my heartbeat quicken. *Couldn't we stay here just a bit longer and talk? Why did we have to go? How could I leave him here on his own?* I knew that if I got up and left, then that was it. *How could I get up and walk out of the room, knowing that he would never be coming home again?*

Two weeks later…

I looked down at the beautiful flower in my hand as I blinked back the tears that so desperately wanted to fall from my eyes. I still couldn't believe that today had finally arrived. It only felt like yesterday that I was holding a whole bouquet of beautiful flowers whilst I proudly married my husband. It felt so unfair that fourteen months on, I was holding a single red rose that was soon to be placed in his coffin. They say that funerals are meant to help bring you acceptance. I didn't feel ready to accept what had happened, and I certainly didn't feel ready to say goodbye.

I was aware of the car engine, and I could hear the music which my cousin had chosen for our journey. He turned to me and smiled, 'Is playing house music okay, Vim? He'd approve of this, wouldn't he?' I nodded and tried to smile as I gazed out of the passenger window. As we began our 20-mile journey to my in-laws' house, I drifted off into my own world.

The last two weeks had passed by in a daze. On the day my husband passed away, my brother had to physically help me to leave the hospital. I just wanted one more minute, just one more second to be with him. I had sat in the car and started to text my friends to say, *He's left me.* I couldn't say the words, 'he's died' out loud, let alone see them in writing, but I didn't know what else to do. In my head I was convinced I was coping okay, but when I apparently started sending random messages my brother took my phone off me. I know now he was trying to look after me, but at the time I was so confused. I thought I was fine, but I guess I was still in shock. One minute I was watching television and having a cup of tea, the next minute I was watching my husband fight for his life. How do you even begin to deal with something like that?

After we drove back from the hospital, my sister-in-law had come back to my flat with me. I walked in and thought, *Oh, his stuff is all here.* I had no idea what I was going to do with everything; I just knew I needed to pack a bag, as I was going to stay at my dad's house. I thought I'd just be there for the night and that I'd come back in the morning, but my sister-in-law asked me to pack for a few days. She had to help me choose what to take, as nothing made sense and I was finding it hard to think straight. I did choose to take something my husband had bought me. I picked it up and held it close, not wanting our memories to fade. I felt scared that I'd forget the times we'd shared, now he was gone. *Was he really gone?* It felt so surreal, as though I could still wake up at any given moment. Despite how hard

I wished for it be a horrible nightmare, the reality was that the next time I came home, he wouldn't be here. He would never be here again, from now on it would just be me.

When I arrived at my dad's house, everything was so hazy. On the drive there I had tried to make my brain remember everything about my husband. I wanted to hear his laugh; I wanted to see his smile. I reminisced about a time when we were dating, when we had watched a film together at the cinema. In my mind, it was one of those films where I could have happily had a power nap and woken up at the end; in my husband's mind, it was the most hilarious film he'd ever seen! I remember looking over at him whilst he was laughing so hard. He had been so full of joy that I couldn't help but smile, too. At the time, I had no idea that we wouldn't be gifted years of these special moments, but I still remember wanting to capture and remember that moment like a photograph imprinted in my heart. I wanted to remind myself of all of these little moments, but it was as though my brain was shutting down. Maybe it was trying to protect me from the hurt. I was still in shock and couldn't believe this had happened to me.

Over the next few days, I remember being told that I needed to eat and that I needed to sleep. I had no appetite and had to force myself to eat, but I had no problems sleeping. Not only did I feel physically exhausted all the time, but sleep was my only way of escaping from the world that I was readjusting to living in. I loved that when I was asleep, I didn't have to think, I didn't have to make any decisions, and I didn't have to feel my pain. Well, that was until I woke up. My body would lie so peaceful and still, in between being fast asleep and being ready to wake up. Just for a moment, just one tiny little moment, there would be a sense of calm. And then BAM! There was that gut-wrenching moment of remembering the reality of what had happened. The pain would then rush back into my heart whilst a million and one thoughts would rush back into my head.

The first few days were the hardest. I wanted to sleep all the time, but I couldn't stay asleep for very long. My dad asked the doctor to visit me at home, and he asked if they could prescribe me some sleeping tablets. I was reluctant to take them, along with the antidepressants he also prescribed me. I told them both I wasn't taking them. The doctor tried to explain logically how the tablets would help me to cope with my emotions, but I mustered all my strength and told him no. I said I didn't need a chemical to help me, I would deal with it all head-on, and I would do this by myself. I could tell my doctor didn't really understand, but in my head it was clear. I kept telling myself: *I've got to get through this, and I will get through this.*

I must say right now, there is absolutely nothing wrong with taking anti-depressants or any medication to support you with self-regulating emotions. The way the doctor explained it to me made perfect sense. The way I understood it to be was this. Right then, my happy levels were low but over time the happy levels in your brain increase; the anti-depressants just make you get there quicker. My fear was when I stopped the tablets – because I knew I would – would the happy levels not drop? *How would I bring myself back up again? Did I need to go through that, or could I just do it now?* I knew my way would take longer, but I also knew that deep down I had the strength to take the longer path. So that was that. I didn't want medication. I was going to do everything it took to raise my happy levels on my own. I was going to do it my way. What I didn't know was that this experience would form the root of my journey of discovering who I was, and my purpose in life.

'Earth to Vimi. Earth to Vimi! You look like you were in your own little world then. We're nearly there, are you okay?' I nodded to my cousin and took a deep breath. I was as ready as I was ever going to be…

A message to my younger self…

If I could go back in time and speak to my younger self, I'd want to tell her that there is no correct way to go through this. You are going to have some really, really shit days. Days where you feel like you're clawing the walls and can't breathe, and the pain is unbearable. You will have never felt pain like it. It's like your heart is breaking. BUT – and there is a BUT – you WILL be ok. You will get through it and you will, in time, heal. It will take a lot of self-reflection, a lot of inner strength, but if you face it head-on and want to drag yourself out of the dark place you are in – you will get through it.

I wish I had known that my confidence would be rocked to its core. That I would get pangs of pain when people celebrated things that I didn't have a chance to. I wish I'd known that it was ok and that it's just life. I wish I'd known that if I loved myself enough, I would get through anything. I wish I'd known that if I invested in and learned to love me, then nothing would break me.

Being able to survive everything I went through

showed me that I am resilient and mentally strong, and I am enough to get me through anything that life throws at me.

It has taught me that I should never give up.

It has taught me the value of people and life and not to take anything for granted. I take pictures to remember memories and feelings. I also take a snapshot in my mind of moments, sounds, and laughter, so that I can lock it away and dip into my mind when I want. It may be a coping mechanism for future loss, but I have accepted that, and it gives me peace knowing that I've mindfully acknowledged the precious moment in front of me.

It has taught me that when we are old it won't matter how many break-ups or separations we've had, tears we've shed, or people we have lost along the way during our journey. What will matter are memories, experiences, shared stories and tales. What will matter is when we reach for that cup of tea and close our eyes, we are catapulted back to precious moments of when we shared a cup of tea with our loved ones.

I now feel emotionally strong.

If you are going through a similarly hard time right now, know that you are not defined by your circumstances or your situation. You are not a label. You are in a transformation phase of the next version of an improved you. Embrace the journey as much as you can, know that you will always get to where you are supposed to go; and know that if you're not there, it's not the end.

I am me and proud of it.

I am The Girl Who Refused to Quit.

Dedication

To my dad, who taught me never to give up, and my mum Leela, in spirit, who showed me to be brave and courageous and to dance even though you're the only one on the dance floor!

About the Author

Vimi is from the UK and is a motivational speaker and business owner. She holds women empowerment groups and events, and welcomes inspirational people to contact her to be part of these events and groups. She is passionate about empowering people to be the best version of themselves despite their circumstances and life experiences. Her life experiences have brought her to where she is today, and she often follows her instinct through life as she believes that you are at your happiest when you follow your passion. She's intuitive, resilient, and spiritual.

Contact

www.mysolutionwellbeing.com
info@mysolutionwellbeing.com
Instagram: the_root_room

Vimi will be publishing her first book, *Light After Dark – A true story of love and loss,* in 2020.

The Beauty of Trauma

Kathy Watters

'I'm sorry, but there is no hope,' said the nurse. She'd just told me that, at almost 12 weeks pregnant, my baby's heartbeat was slow and it was unlikely that he would survive. I tried to take in what I had just been told, but it didn't make any sense. I wanted to scream that as a mother I couldn't and wouldn't give up hope on my child. But the words wouldn't come. I was told that it was just a matter of time, and to carry on as normal. It was even suggested that I return to work if I wanted. I could barely make it to the door past the hospital waiting room, never mind return to work. I was steadily losing blood. My head was like Clapham Junction and my legs felt like they could buckle at any moment. Could this all be for real? It felt so wrong.

Two nights passed before I was rushed to hospital with intense bleeding and pain. As I lay in the hospital bed, still praying for a miracle, I stared out of the window and across at the opposite corridor. My eyes were drawn to the most beautiful pair of framed angel wings which hung on the wall, and a large gold cross which shone bright. I reckoned the prayer room must have been located somewhere within that part of the hospital, and enjoyed the stillness of the moment as I admired their beauty. I have always been very intuitive and open to guidance in the form of signs, messages, and dreams. These spiritual experiences have helped me through some of the most difficult times of my life.

I felt a huge wave of peace flow though me and was sure that these were signs that all was going to be okay. I drifted into a deep sleep and woke again the next morning to realise that right then all was far from okay. I told my husband what I had seen the night before, but then I looked across the corridor and realised that neither the angel wings nor the cross were there. *Had I imagined them?* They had looked and felt so real.

A short while later, another scan confirmed that my baby had not survived, and I was no longer pregnant. None of it made any sense. I felt empty. I felt numb. I felt like my baby had been robbed from me in the night. Nothing that anyone said eased my pain.

The burial service didn't take place for another three weeks, and was on the same day as our second wedding anniversary. I found that time between death and burial really tough. I couldn't shake off the fact that our baby was lying alone in a mortuary, whilst others either avoided us or tried to comfort us with what felt like the least consoling words. Comments like, 'Sure, aren't you lucky you have a daughter?' and 'You can try again', or 'At least it happened early', and 'Maybe it was for the best'.

It's true that we did have our eldest daughter at the time and felt very blessed to have her in our lives, but that still didn't take away from the loss I felt for my son. I say 'son', not because we were told that I was carrying a boy, but more of an intuitive feeling I had. At the burial service, the hospital chaplain, the Reverend Jones, encouraged us to trust whatever gender we felt was right for our baby and, more importantly, to name him. This, he explained, would help us to mourn our loss and talk about him more easily.

It was an interdenominational service for babies who had died within the first trimester of pregnancy. Alongside other grieving parents, we laid our 12 babies to rest in the tiniest white coffins to share the same grave. Reverend Jones spent time with me and my husband, comforting us with his words and pastoral advice. Then along came the next shockwave.

Just five days later, we learned that Reverend Jones, a diving enthusiast, was tragically killed in a diving accident off the coast of Donegal. And not just any place off the coast of Donegal, but the exact spot where my husband and I spent days on end when we first started dating. It was the place where we had the photographs taken for our engagement photo shoot, and where we went for solace to cope with our loss and grief. To have met Reverend Jones for the first time at our son's burial only days before his own death and at a place that holds such significance for us, was startling. It was another reminder – not that I felt I needed one – of how precious life really is, and how quickly it can be taken away. We were some of the last, if not the last, mourners that he comforted before facing his own death. Somehow, his words about finding strength after the loss of a loved one and the importance of keeping their memory alive had more of an impact now, and would continue to do so – even to the present day.

Grieving and still in shock, I tried to process our loss

and the unshakeable guilt that our son's death was my fault. Eight months earlier, there had been a court case which, after more than 18 months of legal proceedings, resulted in a conviction and prison sentence for someone who had sexually abused me and others as children. The sentence served as a form of justice and gave me a great sense of relief to speak out after over 20 years of keeping 'the secret' largely to myself. Being a firm believer in mind/body connection, I couldn't help but wonder if the stress of the trial and the fact that I had sought very little therapeutic help to deal with my past trauma, had caused me to miscarry. I blamed myself for not doing enough to properly heal and free myself from the shackles of my past.

I was angry that just when my whole life seemed to be on the up, it was now spiralling downhill once more. I had a professional social work career, was happily married, and had welcomed our first-born daughter Lara into the world. *How many times*, I wondered, *did God want me to hit rock bottom? Was it not enough that I had lived through and survived the heavy weight of childhood trauma which permeated my everyday life?* The flashbacks. The feelings of shame and guilt that I carried for so long. My childhood innocence robbed. Broken trust shattered into millions of pieces. A lifetime of hurt, confusion, and fear. Always feeling like I was never good enough. Not pretty enough. Not smart enough. Not talented enough. Just never enough. All of which spilled into my relationships, including a very abusive and toxic one, which for a time validated all of the inadequate feelings I held about myself. The end of that relationship was followed by a period of depression, along with suicidal thoughts.

It was in my twenties that I hit one of my lowest points and had a profound spiritual experience which convinced me not to act on my thoughts. I received a clear message that it was not my time to go and that I had other things yet to fulfil. I had no clue what it meant, but I trusted what I felt at the time. So, I knew I didn't feel depressed or suicidal like I had back then. But I was grieving, and I did feel angry.

Losing our son brought home to me how precious life is and how quickly it can end. It made me realise that I had spent most of my life cocooned in fear, pushing down the pain of my past, and I no longer wanted to live that way. All the feelings that lay dormant in me started to rise up. It was like a tiny spark deep inside had ignited and raged into a fierce fire, which was rising up and bellowing its way out of me. There was no holding it back, and I no longer even wanted to. Through the depths of my grief emerged a determination like never before. I was ready for change.

I began to realise that speaking out about my childhood trauma was only the beginning of my healing journey, when for so long I had thought that it would be the end. But it was only now, after the loss of our son, that I was ready and determined to heal in every way I could. I felt like a force to be reckoned with, and even though my heart was sore from grief, I no longer felt afraid. I was determined to make our son's life count. I was ready and willing to make the rest of my life the best of my life. I wanted to be the best mum and role model that I could be to our eldest daughter and our daughters that were yet to come.

I had known about the Law of Attraction and the work of Louise Hay for many years at that point, and had already experienced many benefits of working with these Universal

Laws and teachings. But now, I was ready to take life to a whole new level. I set out my intentions to God and the Universe and I made it clear that I expected them to be met or better. I wanted to heal at the deepest level possible so that nothing from my past could hold me back any longer.

The days and months that followed were full of signs, synchronicities and, to be honest, miracles. It was like gates had opened in front of me and into my life flooded people, experiences, healing, opportunities, and solutions to challenges in my life. I leaned into what intuitively felt right, and it was then that the Law of Attraction seemed to propel into action like never before. To help with my grief, I travelled to West Sussex on an Arvigo womb healing retreat. This led me to studying and becoming a bio-energy therapist and Louise Hay 'Heal Your Life' teacher, along with several other coaching and wellbeing certifications. And all of this was within a year of losing Angel and during my pregnancy with our second daughter Bella.

Little did I know that having first discovered the work of Louise Hay 10 years earlier, when her book fell off a shelf in front of me, I would later be certified in her teachings. All the pieces of my life puzzle were starting to make sense, and I realised that I had been given the signs for many years to lead me into the work I do now as an Empowerment coach. After completing my bio-energy course, the 'Heal Your Life' training course was a significant investment. I was heavily pregnant, yet I knew I had to do it. With the final payment date looming and no idea how I would pay for the course, my employer overpaid me for the first time ever by the exact amount I needed. We reached an agreement whereby I would repay the amount interest-free over two years! Alongside this, I experienced profound healing during one of my bio-energy training sessions which, at five months pregnant, cleared me of the severe pregnancy nausea and sickness I had suffered throughout my first pregnancy. Had there been any doubt in my mind about the incredible power of energy healing and the ability of our bodies to heal using this modality, I had none whatsoever after this experience.

I was going with the flow of life and paying attention to the signs, whilst enjoying the magic and miracles that came my way. I felt the presence of my son Angel willing me on, as I still do. Life felt good, and just two years after losing Angel, we were blessed with another two daughters. Born less than a year apart, they are what we refer to in Ireland as Irish twins. Had Angel not gained his wings when he did, we wouldn't have our two youngest daughters in our lives.

Starting a business with three kids aged three and under may not seem like the best timing, but it all just seemed to unfold that way. I needed case studies as part of my training courses, and after people found that they were benefiting from sessions, they recommended me to others and word soon spread. Having struggled myself for so long, I loved being able to help empower others to overcome challenges and live life in a better way.

But just as one part of my life was blossoming, another part came crashing down. My husband, who I was completely devoted to, called time on our marriage. Although I tried desperately to keep our little family together, it just wasn't to be. I was heartbroken. It was rejection again, and all the feelings of not being good enough came flooding back, along with the hurt, betrayal, and deceit. I had to once more break to my parents the crushing reality of my broken life. Only this time it wasn't just about me, but my daughters, too. The saving grace in all of it were the words of my father. As he breathed a sigh of relief and his voice trembled, he said, 'Thank Christ, I thought you were going to tell me you had cancer.' And as devastated as I was about my marriage collapsing, his words rang true. I would come through this, and there were yet again much worse things that I could have been faced with.

Just weeks before Christmas in 2017, I set up a new home with my three young daughters and took complete time out from my business. It was time to practise what I preach, by taking care of myself and my family first. It also gave me the space to reflect. *Why was I still not enough?* When I eventually found out the truth, through oceans of tears, I made myself a solemn promise to never ever doubt my intuition again.

During this time out from my business, I wasn't sure if I wanted to continue with empowerment coaching when my own life seemed like one big car crash after another. *Who was I to coach people on living their best life when my own seemed like one huge mess?* Yet this new wave of trauma helped connect me with an even greater band of women who reached out to me for support. Several months after my marriage broke down, they told me that they admired my strength and needed my help to work through the ending of their own marriages and relationships. They had seen strength in me which I did not feel for myself at the time, and I quickly reminded them that I was not actively working. However, after months of repeated requests, I chose to recognize these as signs to follow, and business resumed.

And that's the thing with life. None of us ever have it all figured out, and I'm not even sure that we're supposed to either. There will always be challenges and roadblocks along the way. Sometimes we are forced to take time out as a result of illness, loss, or some form of trauma. But it's knowing that there is always a way through and that you can and must get back up again. Rather than trying to reach that elusive state of happiness all of the time, I empower others to love and accept themselves as they are. By being really honest with ourselves about how we feel, we can learn from our individual experiences and discover how to heal from deep within. By connecting with our soul truth, we can ignite the inner power that lies within each of us to pursue our dreams and get what we really want from life.

I no longer wish to have someone else's life, as I did so many times before, and I strongly advise against this to everyone reading this. There were several people who, completely unaware of how I was really feeling, told me when I was at my lowest point that they wished they were me and had my life. So, let that sink in. You truly never know what anyone else is battling in their life.

I used to try and hide the pain of my trauma by keeping it all inside; now I embrace all the bits of me that I thought were broken, and am filled with pride. For all of my broken bits have made me who I am, and I've learned more about myself in piecing my parts back together again than most people ever get to learn about themselves in a lifetime. Life can be really tough sometimes, and there's no denying that. Trauma is not something that any of us consciously choose, yet it is something that we all experience. The challenges will continue, however it is how we choose to respond to each challenge and traumatic event that counts.

Trust that you will find a way through and each time rise stronger than before. There is always, always a way. The life lessons won't always come immediately, but they will come. Whether you choose to recognize them or not, is entirely your choice. Sometimes it is our darkest moments that awaken our greatest potential. And that, for me, is the beauty of trauma!

A message to my younger self...

If I could go back in time and speak to my younger self, I'd hold her tight and whisper in her ear, 'Trust me when I say that this pain and fear you feel will ease. You will find the peace and happiness that you seek. You don't need to worry about how it will happen; just trust that it will. Bit by bit, you will discover a new way to live and love life. Keep believing in miracles, because some pretty big ones are on their way to you. Amongst them you will be blessed with the most beautiful children, who will teach and enrich your life so much. You will be a shining light for many trying to find their way out of the darkness. Yes, YOU! This is my solemn promise to you.'

I wished I'd known that the person I was searching for all along to free me from my pain, was me. I spent so much of my life seeking guidance and answers outside of myself, when all that I was searching for was already inside of me waiting to be discovered.

Being able to survive everything I went through gave me a glimpse of my inner strength and how unlimited the potential of each and every one of us truly is. Instead of feeling fearful and never enough, I learned to accept myself, face the things that scared me the most, and rise to new challenges.

I have learned many lessons along the way and I'm still learning, as we all are. The grief and loss of losing my son 'Angel' led me towards the path of setting myself free. Becoming my own best friend, promising to never doubt my intuition again, doing more things that excite me, taking risks, stepping out of my comfort zone, making the most of every single day, and following my own truth, are some of the key lessons.

I now feel so proud of myself and all that I have overcome. I see and appreciate the world in a completely different way. I feel truly free to be me.

If you're going through a similarly hard time right now, please believe me when I say that there is always a way through. I know it might feel like there's not right now, but if I can do it, I know you can, too. And just like the message that I received, let this be your sign that it's not your time to give up either.

I am the proud hero to that frightened little girl inside of me, the confused teenager, and the desperate young adult that was waiting to be freed. I have unlocked the power that lies within each of us to live life lit.

I am The Girl Who Refused to Quit.

Dedication

For Angel; you gained your wings to help set me free. The bond between mother and child will never sever. I will hold you in my heart forever.

About the Author

Kathy Watters is an Empowerment Coach who hails from the lakeland County of Fermanagh in Northern Ireland, where she continues to live with her three daughters.

Whilst currently on a break from Social Work, and when not actively working with coaching clients, she can be found daydreaming about what she wishes to manifest next, writing, enjoying long soothing walks in the countryside, or going on mini adventures with her daughters.

Having navigated her way through many of life's ups and downs on her journey of self-discovery and transformation, it is her mission to empower others to create a life they love, ignite their intuition, and thrive.

Contact

Facebook: kathywatterscoach
Instagram: @kathywatterscoach
www.kathywatters.com
kathy@kathywatters.com

The Grief Effect

Bibian Green

What the hell is going on? What am I meant to think? I have just received a Facebook message from my nephew to say there's bad news in Zambia. *Bad news? What does that mean? Has something happened to Dad? Is it Dad? Oh my God! Is Dad okay? I mean, yeah, he's survived two strokes, but why hasn't anyone told me what's going on? Why hasn't he got back to me? Maybe everything is okay now? Oh my God, why won't anyone call me, what am I going to do?*

Two hours of panic passed, and I still hadn't heard anything. I was alone in Dubai with my son, and we were meant to be going to the water park for the best day of our holiday. I had a feeling that something awful had happened, but why wouldn't anyone tell me?

Then I received a call from my sister. I couldn't understand the words that she was saying. She was screaming, wailing, and crying! I was trying to make sense of it all, but it was like an echo coming through the phone and I thought she said something like, 'Pascal is dead.' But that couldn't be right. Not my brother, NO!

Have you ever felt like your legs were going to collapse beneath you with shock? That's what I wanted to do, but in reality, I needed to put one foot in front of the other and make sure that my son enjoyed his time at the water park, because that's what mothers do. How could I explain to a ten-year-old who was just about to go on one of his dream adventures that his uncle was dead?

On the 26th October, 2018, my life unexpectedly changed in ways words can never describe. The shock of my brother's death emotionally collapsed me. The weird thing was, before travelling to Dubai, I had thoughts about inviting Pascal to meet us there, but for one reason or another, I never suggested the idea to him. From that moment on, I got stuck on emotional rewind and failed to move forward. I replayed moments of regret whenever his photos popped up on my phone, and I felt a lump in my throat. Life seemed to move in painfully slow motion; it was like waking up from one of those bad dreams. But I wasn't dreaming. Three days later, I flew back home to England.

Although I was close to my brother, his death and funeral happened many thousand miles away in Zambia. I could not attend the funeral, but I watched it on Facetime. I remember the open casket at the cemetery, and everyone gathered around the grave to sing and say their last goodbyes. Suddenly, the casket slowly went down into the earth. My heart stopped. A part of me was leaving me forever. I fell on my husband and cried with distress. He could feel my pain. For a long time, I had kept it trapped inside me, but all these emotions were now coming out.

I could not support my body, and my husband held me like a baby. I had no control of my body. I wanted to die. I wanted to take my brother's place. I wanted him to be where I was. No, I could not accept his death. But, even worse, I could not deny it any more; his body had been buried while I watched on my iPhone. I had to live with it – live a life I was not ready for. I don't remember how I managed to watch the whole burial; I just knew I was not going to be the same any more. I had lost a part of myself.

Though I mentally pushed the loss out of my mind and tried to continue with my business and life as usual, my body would not let me. I was left with an overwhelming feeling of sadness in my heart like I had never felt before.

I was no stranger to loss, but this felt so painful. I had learnt that people who lose their siblings are the most sadly forgotten. And it is hard to find help, since there are not a lot of experts on sibling loss. Pascal had been in my life for 45 years. When I had concerns about life, he would be there to listen to me. If I was crying, he would give me a hug and cry with me. Whenever I visited Zambia, he would be at the airport waiting for me. He was simply the kindest and funniest big brother. He was the one with whom I could disagree and still love with all my heart. Losing my brother made me lose my joy. How could I have joy if I had lost a part of me?

I used to be a girl who smiled constantly. When he died, I truly believed that I did not deserve to be happy. I felt that if I smiled, I'd be betraying my brother. I felt selfish every time I had fun. Every birthday, he used to call me to wish me a happy birthday, but that year I had not picked up or returned his call because I was too busy with work. I regret this immensely. I felt like I deserved to grieve for all of my life.

I isolated myself for several months. Instead of accepting

my pain, I turned it into frustration, and for a long period of time, I was hypervigilant and lost trust in people. I was scared of everything. I was terrified of driving. I was scared of being killed, scared of being attacked. I would wake up from having a nightmare and fear something bad was going to happen, or that I would be involved in some terrible accident. Even during the day, I was experiencing fears of death. I realised that I could be taken at any moment, at any age, without any signs.

I lived with this inexplicable fear for a while, unable to tell anyone. Then the fear turned into sadness, and the sadness turned into loneliness. Suddenly I had severe physical pain, tension in my shoulders, neck and back, jaw clenching, headaches, IBS, weight gain, insomnia and fatigue. It felt like a fight to be happy; anxiety and emptiness became my struggle. I used to be so strong and happy, but after Pascal's death I lost a sense of who I was. My husband didn't know how to comfort me; he felt helpless. Some people expected me to 'get over it' very quickly, but I did not want to burden anyone by sharing my pain. Instead, I found safety in confining myself to my bedroom, sobbing my eyes out day in, day out. I didn't want to face people. I had a 'why bother' attitude, a lack of energy, drive, and motivation. I became very forgetful and snappy. I didn't want to leave the house, wore the same dark baggy clothes day and night, and went for days without having a bath or shower. The upstairs of my house was looking like one of those hoarders' TV programmes, with clothes strewn everywhere. My house was a tip and my head was a mess.

My friends on social media missed my motivational posts and wondered where 'bubbly Bibian' had gone. I wished I knew. I was barely getting two hours sleep each night and I couldn't function.

My life became consumed with painkillers, therapists' and doctors' appointments. Countless blood and hormone tests were carried out, and everything was normal. *How could that be possible?* Through my tears, I begged my GP to tell me why I was in so much pain and not getting any sleep. I felt hopeful when she signed my prescription, but when I showed the tablets to my chiropractor, she shook her head in disapproval and said, 'Bibian, I cannot believe you have been prescribed Amitriptyline!' She showed me my MRI scan results which indicated a high score for shoulder, neck, and back muscle tension. No wonder I was in so much pain. 'Bibian, you may need to evaluate all areas of your life to identify where your stress is coming from and find a safe space to process what is going on internally,' she advised. 'Have you looked into counselling?'

I looked at her in horror and told her that my business was really busy, I had no time to get stressed. On my way home, I stopped in a lay-by, took my wig off, and cried my eyes out! So many questions ran through my mind. I didn't want to believe that I was stressed. No way, stress was not for strong women like me! But deep down, I knew something had to change. I had not been truly happy in my work life for a while and I had looked at other opportunities, but I feared change.

My husband tried to cheer me up. We travelled to some of the most beautiful holiday destinations on the planet, but I still came back feeling miserable. My eldest son got great grades and left to go to university at Oxford, I had every reason to be happy, yet I still felt empty.

I had two minor car accidents in one week, due to lack of concentration. I consistently made poor decisions. I lost control of my life, and my anxiety became unbearable. I was going through the motions, yet lacking focus and direction. I was successful, yet I was not happy. I had this deep desire for more, yet I was racked with guilt, feeling so ungrateful for what I already had. But one thing I did know was that I didn't want to waste what was left of my life.

Then one morning, I opened Facebook and saw a sponsored advert that looked like it was directed at me. I opened the post and liked what I read. I contacted Dawn, a local counsellor, for a free one-hour 1-2-1 consultation. Dawn helped me to understand what was going on with me. It became apparent that I was carrying a lot of unresolved emotional trauma, and she described the constant muscle tightness I have suffered with for some time as armouring. I had not heard it described this way, but it made perfect sense. She explained that my body was being continually braced for something – a correct description – and was a symptom of my hypervigilant state that always assumes, subconsciously, that I need to be prepared for trauma. In the case of my body, I always have my armour on. It's no wonder my doctor thought I needed Amitriptyline.

I had been through so much shit since birth, and my body had done a damn good job of protecting me up to this point. But I realised my body had reached its limit. The anxiety and pain were signals that there were some things underneath to explore.

I was sick of feeling sick all the time, and my head felt like a pressure cooker about to blow up. As soon as I understood what was happening to me internally, I refused to take medication and quickly started my counselling sessions with Dawn. It was the first time I had ever opened up to someone about all the heinous abuse, grief, and stress I had been through.

I felt lighter after each session, but two days or so later the pains would be back and severe. Dawn said, 'Imagine you are opening wounds that you band-aided for so many years. The pains will get worse before you feel better. Healing takes time.' And it did indeed feel like shit before I began to feel better. After a number of therapy sessions, inner child work, self-help books and YouTube videos, I finally had a deeper understanding of what was happening to me. I started applying what I was being taught, and slowly started to feel better. I was opening up a lot more, and I was shocked at how much I had subconsciously blocked out. It kind of felt like a veil had lifted and I was seeing more than I used to see. Despite having a history of abuse, significant losses, and several other factors that had contributed to my physical pain, it's only been in the past few months that I have become aware of the connection between the two.

In December 2018, I travelled to Zambia and visited my brother's grave. It was very hard for me to accept it was him buried there. How quickly life can change. He was buried next to my mum and my other siblings. At the age of 54, he was gone – it's true that all of the good ones are taken way too soon. I got to see the forensic pathology report which confirmed his cause of death. And this was one of the most difficult visits to Zambia; it triggered all sorts of emotions.

After returning to the UK, I felt that my friends wanted things to get back to normal, and were willing me to 'move on'. I understood what was happening; this is social convention, right? You get a few weeks to grieve, but then it's time to 'get over it', time to get better. Before this loss, I was one of those people. I had no idea of the ways in which grief strips you of who you are and forces you to re-think your entire being.

I attended a business meeting at which someone said something that made me think of my brother – so I mentioned my memory. The atmosphere changed and I saw, out of the corner of my eye, one colleague roll their eyes! I barely spoke for the rest of the meeting. It was then I realised that, except for a very few close friends and family, society had now had enough of my grief. My time in the 'grief sin bin' was up. I fought a battle constantly between what I thought I should do and what I actually wanted to do. I put my 'happy mask' on every time I went out of the front door and I tried to engage in life, but I couldn't keep it up for long. It was exhausting. I was not strong enough to maintain this approach, and every time I was alone, I crumbled. The alternative option, however, was one of isolation and loneliness. Friendship groups changed and separated into those who had suffered a traumatic grief and those who hadn't. I felt like I had become a member of an exclusive grief club – but I didn't want to join. And the price I paid for membership was way too high.

This rollercoaster of emotions continued for a long time. I was often confused. I desperately wanted to 'figure it out' and understand the great meaning so that somehow, I could experience peace and love in my own heart again.

Eventually, I opened up and spoke very, very honestly about it. I began to realise that if I trust that everything happens for a reason, death is not excluded from that. While it was painful to lose my brother in his physical form, there are countless miracles that have happened since his passing.

I now see that it was simply time for his spirit to move on from the body he was in. His spirit is still very much alive to this day, and I experience evidence of that regularly. The key is for me to stay open to see it.

This inner knowing brought a different kind of peace and understanding than I had ever experienced in life.

Continuing with my business in the weight loss industry seemed to me the only path. Most clients I saw had similar stories. It was clear to me that everyone was grieving some kind of loss in their life and turning to food for comfort. I made the decision to cut back on my workload, but this relief was overshadowed by a huge cloud of emptiness that enveloped my being. It prompted the question: what next? Was this all there was to life? Surely there must be more meaning to life than this.

Over the months that followed, the sadness would come in waves. One morning I would be happy and pain-free, but by the evening I would be a mess. I couldn't stand any noise, bright lights, or anyone texting or calling me. I wanted to be left alone. One night, I woke up in tears from a dream that was too realistic for me to keep to myself. In the dream, Pascal was in tears. He apologised for leaving so soon. He warned us about people who were never there for him when he was alive but were there at his funeral. He told me that we would never see him again, that he was gone for good.

His death forced me to view life from a different perspective and set me on a journey to discovering myself and what I was created to do. I didn't want to fix the wrong in people's lives. But there was a purpose for my pain. Not only to help people, but I believe God has a way of telling you that you are headed in the wrong direction, and my pain and anxiety were his way of setting me straight.

Finally, after many months of emotional and spiritual exploration, I discovered The Grief Recovery Method. Through completing The Grief Recovery Method, I faced all the losses. I acknowledged, accepted, apologised where necessary, forgave where necessary, and I came to a place of peace. I also learned to accept that I was hurt and not to hide my pain. Everyone grieves differently. Our society expects us to have a limited grief and to move on within a certain amount of time. People forget that grieving can be a process expended through a lifetime.

A year after my brother's loss, I am still recovering from his death, but I have learned to live without him day after day.

I have realised that there is actually so much beauty in grief. It helps us to realise just how enormous our love can be, which is ultimately why it can hurt so intensely to say goodbye to that person in the form that we knew them.

I wanted to make something out of this experience which pushed me not to give up. I have now trained as a Grief Recovery specialist, and I truly hope my brother would be proud!

A message to my younger self...

If I could go back in time and speak to my younger self, I would tell her, 'I am sorry you were abandoned. You didn't deserve to be called names and put down so often. You didn't deserve any of the abuse or the bullying you went through. The ones who should have protected you, violated you. It was never your fault. You were innocent. You did nothing wrong. You deserved to be cherished and seen for the beautiful treasure you are. You are so smart, lovely, and kind. You are so beautiful inside and out. I am so glad you were born and brought into this world. You have so much to offer. You are so strong. Everything you feel right now is okay. It's okay to cry. You deserve so much better. I will never leave you. I am always here if you need me. You are never alone.'

I wish I had known that when the grief process is stalled, it can take its toll on you. Embrace the emotions you are feeling, and don't be afraid to admit it. It's okay not to be okay. Seek support and professional help as soon as possible. Be good to yourself and take each moment at a time; grief is a natural process that is our human way of emotional healing.

I now feel that the journey I have had so far is meant so that I can grow into the person I am meant to be. Someone who can help others along the journey, so they don't have to experience the same pain longer than I did, because there is a quicker way.

If you are going through a hard time similar to this, I want you to know that you have the power to address and change things at the root of it all. Do the inner child work.

I am ENOUGH.

I am The Girl Who Refused to Quit.

Dedication

For all who have experienced grief of all kinds.

About the Author

Bibian lives in the Cotswolds, England. As a Wellness Coach and certified Grief Recovery Method Specialist, Bibian loves helping people to gain control in their lives emotionally, spiritually, and mentally, through private sessions, workshops, groups, writing, speaking, and training seminars. Her sincerity and vulnerability are some of her most amazing assets and they allow her to empower others, even when life is not easy.

She's an amazing philanthropist and a passionate advocate for trauma recovery.

Her mission is to deliver recovery services to the greatest number of people in the shortest amount of time.

Contact

https://griefrecoverymethod.co.uk/bibian/
https://www.facebook.com/bibiangriefrecovery/

How I Found My Strength
Nicola Harvey

My eyes teared up as a sharp knife of realisation stabbed into my tender heart, freefalling into darkness and numbing my emotions. I was collapsing inside but somehow showing nothing on my face, due to the responsibility. Her words stung. 'Why are you not on Jade's pictures, Nicola? Is something wrong at home?' *Where was I? Why was I not there?* The truth staring me in the face shot an arrow right into my heart.

Only moments before…

It was a beautiful day. The kind of days where there was a gentle breeze on a sunny day. A perfect temperature. I was on my way to pick up my curly-haired three-year-old daughter, Jade. She always wore a cheeky smile, and usually dungarees or trousers chosen by her. It was the end of term, and the playgroup was about to break up for summer holidays. So, with my six-month-old daughter Jasmine in her pram, I waited for the opportunity to go in and collect Jade, along with all her recent painting and artwork.

A lovely playleader, Pru, took me to one side. Now, I wasn't expecting any problems, as Jade was mostly a model, albeit young, student. Pru handed me Jade's papers containing colourful pictures, but pulled one picture out and asked me to look at it. Searching for any problems, anxious that Jade might need correcting, I looked intently at the family portrait that she had drawn.

It didn't look too dissimilar to the other pictures, so I wasn't immediately concerned. I saw Jade depicted with curly hair, Jasmine with her bright blonde hair, and Jade's dad with brown hair. Simple but beautiful. I couldn't see what was wrong. But Pru persisted, holding the picture.

'We are concerned that Jade hasn't drawn you within the picture. Is anything wrong at home, Nicola?'

In that immediate moment, my stomach sank to the floor. I became an empty vessel, emotionless and shocked to the core. There was a lump in my throat, my tears were ready to flow, but I immediately became the 'front'. If the truth came out, I was sure my children would be taken away. So, I became what Pru needed to see, and dismissed the absence of me in the picture as just that Jade must have forgotten, she's only three years old, this doesn't indicate anything kind of attitude. It had become so normal to act how a mother should and in the way that was expected of me, that I could click into functioning emotionally 'auto pilot mummy' so quickly.

Little did she know that behind closed doors I was a woman who had been so desperately ill with ante-natal depression that Jade, in her way, had not *seen* her mum in a very long time.

What Jade *had* seen was her mum struggle daily with

simple tasks like getting breakfast, lunch or tea. Most days, she'd seen her crying, sitting at the top of the stairs, tired or sleeping. I wasn't coping and I am sure Jade felt this was partly her fault. Maybe in her three-year-old's mind she didn't see her mum in any way as part of her family. I can certainly vouch for the fact that the very aspect of living was causing me so much distress that I felt a shadow of who I was or who I should be. I felt so useless to myself and to all of those around me, and questioned if they'd all be better off if I wasn't there.

I don't know when my ante-natal depression started; I don't think there was any 'button pressed' or 'hey, I'm now depressed' happened. It was more like a gradual process of things happening, and an accumulation of situations and emotional feelings.

Depression for me began when my then husband went abroad with his squadron to take part in war; there was so much uncertainty leading up to his departure as to what might happen. He had signed his life away, documents like his will had been written, 'upon my death' had been a huge topic of conversation prior to him leaving for who knew how long.

I felt so anxious, and to top this off I remember texting him the good news that I was pregnant with our second child. He didn't reply for days, due to the fact that connection and Wi-Fi were very poor and he had been working such long shifts. He couldn't explain too much what he or they (meaning the Air Force), were doing, but I was aware of what was on the news and could easily imagine what part he was playing within this.

After a few weeks of him being away, the visions started.

I imagined bombs landing on his head as I graphically watched his limbs being torn apart! It would seem obvious to have anxiety whilst your partner was away, so I dismissed it as being normal. But it was impossible to stop these thoughts. They felt and appeared so real, like a film playing out in front of my mind. My visions became unbearable as they progressed. I couldn't shield or close my eyes, and I was frightened beyond belief. I felt powerless and it was soul-destroying. My mind became a torture chamber from which I couldn't escape.

One of my recurring visions featured a clear glass impenetrable wall. The rest of the room was well lit with clinical white walls, and behind this was my beautiful daughter, Jade. Months later, when her sister was born, she was also part of the vision. It started with them calling for me, crying. I would distract them by placing my hand on the glass, and they would mimic from the other side, their cute tiny hands finding mine. But the visions would always progress, and the girls would start to cry, begin to look hungry, cold, and withdrawn. It would then progress to them looking dirty, emaciated, and withering away. I would watch them die in the most graphic way. It was harrowing, but it didn't stop there.

If I got into a car, I could see myself crashing and blood pouring everywhere. If I walked down the stairs, I'd see myself falling and killing my baby. If I walked outside, I'd see a brick falling and splattering my brains. I was constantly watching my worst fears come to life. There was no need to watch horror movies; my worst fears taunted me every day. They started off as a few images a day, but they got worse and worse and I couldn't even pick up a knife to cut an apple without seeing my finger cut off. After a month of my husband being away, I had stopped sleeping. You name it, I tried it, but staying awake into the early hours became normal.

The sheer exhaustion ensured that daytimes felt like extreme torture. I was exhausted; even getting off the sofa caused distress. It was like having the flu a thousand times over. I had no energy and didn't want to get out of bed. I dreaded the moment Jade woke up, as it meant having to think of things to do. One lunchtime, all I could do was make us garlic bread. I could just about cope with getting food from the freezer to the oven and onto the plate. Any other tasks seemed like such hard work. All of the other ideal mothers would freshly prepare vegetables and cook nutritiously organically delectable meals. I was poles apart from Nigella Lawson!

After two months of this, my life felt like it was shattered. I felt such gut-wrenching emotions that I could not cope. The constant tiredness, visions, paranoia, and an overwhelming feeling of being valueless to those around me. I was convinced I was not being a good wife, mother, daughter or friend. I cried most of the day and all of my waking night. Obsessive thoughts were constantly on my mind. I felt sick to my core, accompanied by overwhelming and powerful negative thoughts. I could not cope with what felt like a physical illness. I felt so desperate.

Somehow, I came to the conclusion that the pain was too much, the visions and the desperate feelings made me feel that everyone would be better off without me. I wouldn't call it a cry for help as it was the only thing that seemed logical to me at the time. My self-worth was shattered, my pain was unbearable, and I became convinced that my only way out was to depart from this world. Illogical but real thoughts flooded my mind: my then husband would find a new wife to be everything he needed; my mum and dad would be ok as they had my brother and sister. This was my sense of self at rock bottom.

Jade and my unborn baby, though, were an issue that I could not resolve in my mind. If I committed suicide, then I would effectively be committing murder on my unborn baby. And to leave my beloved Jade would devastate her. Surely, it's better having a bad mother than no mother at all? But if I took her with me, that would be murder. So, I was stuck in absolute desperation, a living hell, not coping with living.

I had painful, soulful love for my daughter and my unborn baby, but no confidence in my ability to care for them. What on earth was going on? Why is it that motherhood can be so punishing? Life was strangling my ability to give and to receive love. My dream to be a perfect mother was shattered, my belief was at rock bottom, and my perspective on life so negative.

A week after my partner returned from his time away, I recognised that something serious was going on and I booked in to see my doctor. She was so sympathetic and helpful. I was offered counselling and therapy and referred to see a psychiatrist, because she didn't know what to prescribe as I was pregnant. Most importantly, I was diagnosed with antenatal depression.

The road to recovery had begun…

Telling everyone should have been easy, but it wasn't. The reactions weren't what I expected. My mum's comment was, 'I couldn't have done any more to help you.' And my partner said, 'I'm not sure why you are the one with the problem when I went away and was at war.'

But the truth is, it wasn't anyone's problem but mine; no-one caused it, no-one was to blame. I became aware that perhaps I was alone on my recovery as the responsibility on others could be something that maybe they shouldn't have to share.

The midwife in all her years of care hadn't dealt with antenatal depression, so she visited me in my lounge, arms folded, and in a puzzled way said she didn't know how to help me. She only asked about my emotions, not symptoms such as tiredness and insomnia, which at that time I didn't know were linked. We didn't talk about my disabling visions either. I didn't think to mention them as I was not asked; it didn't come up. Still, she was a nice lady.

The only appointment to see the counsellor was during work hours. With my partner, Mum and Dad working full time hours, making an appointment was difficult. Jade was not yet at nursery, so every time I had to find a babysitter. Getting a sitter for the first appointment was difficult, and in the end my partner booked annual leave. I found the session really useful, learning how to talk with positive language and training myself to think positively. But as Jade had to come to my next session and any more thereafter, I decided that it was unfair on her and so I had to stop. I think the counselling was a kind called Cognitive

Behavioural Therapy. I enjoyed the sessions, she was a very caring lady, and by feeling listened to, I found the sessions to have helped with me learning to think in a better for me kind of way.

Walking to the psychiatric department was awkward, as I felt out of place. Even finding the department was a surreal moment. I was 7 months pregnant. I was alone and scared, suspicious that they would section me. No-one reassured me, there was no friendly smile from the receptionists. I just about managed to get my name out when I was asked. A stark grey and green room awaited me. Lots of square chairs in square areas; there were many waiting rooms for differing psychiatric conditions.

I sat down in the waiting room away from people. A scout around confirmed there was no-one scary, but I wasn't in the mood to make polite chat as I was still very anxious. As I sat down, I was handed a clipboard with a couple of questionnaires to fill out. I was now six weeks post diagnosis, so I was feeling a little improved by the emotional support which a diagnosis had given. I think I answered the questions in a more upbeat way, because I was still worried about being taken into hospital. I was then spoken to by a registrar with smooth skin but a very stern face. I was told my results were in! It had felt very much like a test which I would either pass or fail.

Had I really got an illness? Surely not. I was worried that the results may show that I was diagnosed with nothing, but I was also worrying that I was diagnosed with something, too. My thoughts continued racing as I braced myself for the news. The results showed that I had severe antenatal depression. It wasn't a relief; it was a total shock, especially as he emphasised the *severe*. And to be honest, I had thought that I was now ok.

He offered me tablets but couldn't rule out the effects to my baby, so I quickly chose to decline, and he wrote 'against medical advice' on my notes. He was accepting of my decision – I mean, he didn't judge or make me feel awkward about it – and we also discussed how I could help myself without medication. He explained my character, what motivated me and supported my emotions to further give me a good chance of recovery. I asked him if incidents in the past could have created the illness, but he stated absolutely not and snapped, 'It's not good to go over past memories.' That kind of stopped me in my tracks when I was about to talk about an incident when I had been attacked. He clearly was doing his job well, but I didn't understand or know that for sure at the time.

I worked out that maybe a psychiatrist's job wasn't quite what I'd thought. Not much talking therapy. More medicate and keep thoughts to the here and now; I guess, mindfulness. Next, I was taken to see the consultant. Her office was sage green. She smiled nicely, but I didn't totally trust the smile. She asked what I considered to be strange questions and was quite quirky in her ways; she reminded me of a Harry Potter character. I was booked in for a six-week post birth or baby follow up.

I left feeling firstly relieved that I had not been detained, and secondly confused as to why the registrar had been so stern. I'd expected sympathy not sternness. In my super-sensitive place, I didn't understand the motives.

I chose my treatment, and as a duty to myself I recognised that I needed to help me. No-one else could help but me. I had not been good at emotional self-care and never recognised the importance of it. But it was time to take action. I set about helping myself to get better, working out what made me feel good, and came up with a box of treats – initially called my anti-panic box, but latterly called my feel-good box. You may be curious about what was inside it. All things that I loved or made me feel good – lavender oil, Bach flower essence remedy, rose oil, rose quartz crystal, tiger's eye crystal, and hematite crystals. This travelled with me everywhere.

I prescribed myself daily salt baths with Jasmine, and added rose petals. Not choosing medication was against the registrar's point of view, so I needed to work on me. Proving someone wrong was strangely quite inspiring, but there was a very serious side to my actions and I had to acknowledge that. I was a qualified nurse, and knew there was nothing so frustrating as a patient who wouldn't take their medication.

I tried to read research books about my illness – there was some, but many were out of print – and my mum found me a magazine article which helped. Each time I became anxious or felt my thoughts racing, the box came out. Lighting a candle, placing a small amount of lavender oil into my burner, taking Bach flower essence drops, and using my crystals, became the norm.

Jasmine was born at home on a cold November evening. To my relief and shock, she came out very quickly – two hours flat from start to finish! She was very healthy, chubby, and looked beautiful. I couldn't have wished for more.

It was six months later, on that bright and sunny day,

when we picked Jade up from the nursery. The day my heart broke as I was shown a drawing of our family without me in the picture. It had been a whole year of battling with my emotional illness that Jade had witnessed and lived through. I waited for the day that she started to draw me back into her pictures, and it did happen. I'm pleased to report that there was also a smiley face.

I improved slowly, and I mean slowly. The panicky feelings stopped first and I began to cope – that was after the first year. I started to sleep and the visions stopped – that was after the second year. My self-esteem improved, and my sensitivity decreased – probably after the third year. You stop fearing that it will ever happen again after ten years…

It turned out that my marriage wasn't meant to be, but I am now happy and healthy. I am proud to say that Jade is now at university and Jasmine is doing very well at college. I am happy and in love, and my business as a psychic/medium and healer is going from strength to strength. I am forever grateful for my experience, as without it I am sure that I would not be as compassionate and strong as I am today. Appreciating life and what it has to offer has to come with the good bits and the bad bits.

As a medium and healer, I pleaded to those in the spirit world to help me recover. At my worst, I protested how and why I should have to experience an illness like that. It was only after I recovered that they gave me a message:

'Well done, you didn't need our help. You coped and recovered all on your own.'

And that's when the realisation dawned for me that we have the power and ability to transform our lives, recover, renew, reinvent, and most of all to appreciate living.

A message to my younger self...

If I could go back in time and speak to that younger lady, I wouldn't bother to speak to her. It's hard to write, but she wouldn't be in the right place to hear. But I'd make her a cup of tea, sit her on a comfy chair, and just listen. I would allow her to hear her own voice, to work out her own conclusions. I'd empathise and just be with her, holding space as she talked through her experiences, lovingly giving her my time without judgement or a time limit. I would try to get her to understand her own capabilities and strength.

I wish I had known that life can be beautifully challenging. Each crisis, however severe, forms a building block to a stronger personality and contentment. I wouldn't be waiting for someone to make me better or say the right thing, which I think I was for quite some time, as most people around you are going through their own problems, too. I wish I could have seen myself now.

Being able to survive this has taught me that I am an inspirational woman, not that I would want the same experience ever again! I now understand the importance of emotional health – it's as important as physical health. I enjoy knowing my mind and caring for it. It has taught me that although I may feel like giving up, I don't; I get up and keep on going. When you survive, you realise how important you are and that people do care and love you. For my daughters, I strive to be a better person, and I hope that my example encourages them to do the same.

I have learned that anyone has the power to change, and the ability to think positively through a situation. You are strong and you are enough. Little steps each day help;

remember, one step at a time is moving forward. Forgiving yourself, your mind, your hormones for the effects of this illness, is so important. Don't hold onto the guilt that can arise, because you did your best with the effects on the body and circumstances presented to you. Let go of expectation, sometimes 'happily-ever-afters' have to be worked for.

I now feel and am happy and content, but I believe you find it through sadness and a coping system. Having lost it, you definitely search for it. I now have great gratitude that this has not recurred and hopefully never will. I now am qualified in reiki, crystal and colour therapy, aromatherapy, reflexology, and have read many, many self-help books. I have also been able to help many people, all of which I possibly would not have done had I not had my illness and searched for a recovery.

If you are going through ante or postnatal depression, I empathise with you. Do not give up. As long as you are breathing you have the reason to find your strength and work with your personal power. Find your emotional first-aid kit, search for things that help you. Your life, loved ones, and family need you to be present. No-one has or gets an easier ride through life, so live your life to the best of your ability. And most importantly, one day you will feel inside that your smile has come back, and you can appreciate that if ever it goes again it will always return.

I am resilient and strong and appreciate my soul's journey.

I am The Girl Who Refused to Quit.

Dedication

I dedicate my chapter to my daughters Jade and Jasmine, and my partner Chris.

Thank you for being my loving support and inspiration.

About the Author

Nicola Harvey is a spiritual psychic medium who enjoys helping others through uplifting spiritual readings and demonstrations. She loves her work.

Nicola is committed to her own healing, both personal and spiritual development. And through her own experiences in life, she enjoys sharing her wisdom to those it may help. Her mission is to help anyone wishing to develop their own spiritual abilities and self, which she believes is open to all.

She hopes that anyone reading her chapter who has experienced a mental health illness feels hope within her story.

Nicola lives near to Loughborough with her supportive partner and wonderful daughters.

She has been described as a 'gifted light worker'.

Contact

https://www.nicolaharveypsychicmedium.com
https://www.facebook.com/NicolaHarvey2222/
Nicolaharvey2222@gmail.com
https://www.instagram.com/Nicola_harvey_psychic

The Panic

Larissa Martincic

There is something so special about feeling the movement of your unborn child within your body. During my third pregnancy, in the early hours of the morning you could find me in the most peaceful state, enjoying my unborn son AJ's playful and active movements. He would wake me before the birds would begin their sweet music, and this became the most magical part of my day. As I approached my thirty-first week of pregnancy, I was running around after our two young daughters, Miranda (5) and Gabriella (3). Life wasn't easy; however, life was great. I was healthy, happy, and growing bigger by the day.

On this particular day – May 4, 2010 – my day started just like the ones before, but I had no idea that within the next few hours I would be facing every mother's worst nightmare.

I started to make my mental list of my day's tasks and chores. I really wanted to make Miranda's sixth birthday party special for her, because I knew that I would not be able to give her as much attention once the baby came. I began thinking of all the prepping that needed to be done within the next five days. I glanced at the clock and felt a sense of sadness as I became aware that my special time with AJ would be cut short. I paused and thought, *that's weird, he's not his usual active self*. I lay there rubbing my stomach, speaking to him, and encouraging him to wake up. I gave myself extra time because I desperately wanted to feel him moving magically inside of me.

As my husband drank his coffee, I told him that I hadn't felt AJ move yet, but he assured me it was ok, kissed us goodbye, and off to work he went. When I arrived at school, one mom noticed I was not myself. I told her I hadn't felt AJ move yet. She gave me some advice on what to do to get him moving, so I raced home to do just that. As the minutes passed, unease was starting to fill my body. As I lay on the couch, after drinking the largest glass of sugary orange juice, I waited. This was it; this is what AJ needed to wake his sweet little body up. As I waited for what felt like an eternity, I knew in the core of my being that something was wrong.

What I perceived as a slight kick could be compared to a twenty-week flutter, but this movement was my son's fight to live. It was that feeling that let me know in my soul that my son was not ok. I stood up and felt a dampness in my undergarments – not water breaking, no contractions, just something wasn't right.

My heart began to beat faster and my mind started to race. I called the doctor's and they made me an appointment to check the baby to be on the safe side. As the receptionist went to hang up the phone, a feeling came over me that I am unable to put into words. It was a clear knowing that I felt with every part of my body. 'No! Something is very wrong. This is not normal, and I just know this can't wait.' She put me on hold before informing me that my doctor wanted me to go to the hospital. I felt nervous but reminded myself it was a precaution… or so I thought.

When I arrived at the hospital, the nurse began to ask me simple questions as if this was just a routine examination. I was instructed to put a hospital gown on and told they would carry out some checks. We chatted as she placed a monitor on my belly and turned towards the machine.

The second she turned that machine on, the horror of what we heard still plays in my mind. It was sheer static, white noise, and the loudest sound of nothing you could ever imagine. *Where was the heartbeat?* She looked at me; there were no words, just utter panic. The scream that came from my soul was a plea to God as I thought my son had gone! There was no conversation, no explanation, no questions. Lights were flickering, codes were frantically called, and doctors were filling the room with every machine, tool, and all the training needed to respond to a baby with no heartbeat.

I screamed, 'NO, NO, NO! This isn't happening! NO, you have to save him. This can't be. Please, NO, my son, he cannot die. NOOOOOO!!' No-one responded. They were working on me. But I was no longer the patient, my son was. I remember seeing the hospital clock, I could read 11:52 but the tears were coming so fast that my eyes could no longer see the room. One nurse was wiping my tears, another was holding my hand; I was just sobbing.

After what felt like an eternity, I heard the words, 'I got it!' The room fell quiet, and we all froze as my sweet baby's heart beeped across the machine. It was a beautiful sound, but one that they knew was not normal or healthy. The beats that represent the sound of life were very slow, with long pauses in between each one. Then all of a sudden, the line of hope went flat and the machine let out the kind of excruciating sound that nightmares are made of!

The doctor in charge screamed, 'O.R. 3 NOW, we're losing him!' The bed began to move, whilst the doctor was still on it with me. There was no time. We raced out of the room, doors flying open, and all I could see were the fluorescent lights flashing before my eyes. The nurse was asking me my husband's name, his telephone number, when I last ate. No-one was telling me what was happening. There was no time for explanations, my son was dying. I did the one thing that I could; I began to pray. What I felt during those moments could be seen as an out of body experience. My mind was no longer in the present moment, as I went somewhere else. I was screaming out loud to my spiritual protectors and angels. I began to plead with my grandmother to save him. As if she was standing in the room, I was begging her to help him, because in those harrowing minutes I was sure my son was gone.

In the operating room, they got me on the table, and I could hear the loud sounds of the surgical tools hitting the metal tables. I couldn't move but I heard the chaos. The last voice I heard was the command from a doctor to get me under, now! I was trembling. All I could see was this man, face to face with me, wiping my tears as he placed the anaesthesia mask over my face and put me to sleep.

I was helpless the night I heard God.

As I took my first breath, it was like someone was holding me under water and I was being released back into my body. I jumped with such force, as if someone had removed a weight from my chest. It took a few minutes to realize that someone was shaking me. His arms were grabbing my shoulders, shaking and hugging me and yelling my name, all in one motion. I started to focus on the man before me and realised it was my father, giving me the most tender loving embrace a parent could give to their child. As I started to come back to the present reality, I heard, 'Riss, you did it, you did it. He's here, you saved him, honey. He's here, he's alive!' My body went limp, crying tears of fear and pain as I wept in my daddy's arms. I was yelling and crying the same phrase: 'My baby, my baby, where is my baby?'

I began to grasp my stomach and look all around for him, as if someone was going to give him to me and I could wake up from this hell. I couldn't move, and I couldn't comprehend what had happened.

Nothing made sense, I was in a state of shock and just lay in my bed, lifeless. I didn't talk, I didn't ask questions, and as each doctor and nurse would enter the room I just lay in my bed frozen with tears that would not stop streaming down my face. I didn't care or think about a single thing, other than that I needed my son. I didn't see my son for the next nine hours, but I continued to pray and speak to him through my thoughts, telling everyone that he was going to be ok.

The doctor came in and spoke to me, but he could see that my eyes were distant. I just kept shaking my head, and my husband helped me off the bed to take me to our son. To this day, I don't know if we've ever spoken about those moments when our eyes saw AJ for the first time, but I know the fear we both felt. I don't think a parent can truly describe that moment, because I don't believe there are words in our vocabulary to describe what it is like to see your child lifeless and in distress. My son was so tiny, so fragile, wires seemed to be coming from everywhere, and he was lying there so helpless. *How can this be my baby?* I thought. *How can this be happening to him? I've failed him!* He was suffering with every beat his precious heart took. The pain came through every tear I shed, and as my tears fell upon his sweet body, I loved him with every part of my soul. The shock hit me, and I could not stop sobbing. As I placed my hands upon my son, I did the only thing I knew how – I prayed hard.

Later that evening, everyone left so that I could get some sleep, but the only thing I could think of was that my son was fighting for his life. I wanted to be with him so badly, and every muscle in my body ached for him. It is the most unnatural feeling to give birth and not be able to hold your child; it was torture. AJ was still in a critical condition and I was not able to lift him from the machines that were keeping him alive, so holding him was not an option. I did not know it at the time, but our son was what they called a 50/50. The staff had done all they could do medically, and it was now out of their hands whether he made it through the night.

As I lay in bed feeling helpless, I cried and began pleading with God. I wasn't praying like the prayers of the past; I was pouring my soul out to God. I was righting every wrong in my life and promising to make the world a better place. During my conversation with God, my emotions were so raw that I didn't even realise I was shouting, as if I was making sure he heard me. I remember saying the most difficult words a mother could ever say out loud. But I knew I was helpless; I had no control over whether my son lived or died, and I gave my son to God. I knew in that moment that my son was not mine, that he belonged to God and he was not mine to take. Instead of demanding God give me my son, I released my son to God and prayed for his mercy. I told God that if he wanted AJ to remain in heaven, that I trusted that was what was best. But I asked God to make sure AJ would always know how much I loved him and that I would forever be his mother. I asked God that if he believed I could be a good mother to please let AJ stay with us, and allow me the chance to be his mother. Through my tears, I felt a weight lift from my body.

In that that very dark moment, when I realized just how powerless I was, God came to me. I felt his presence fill my soul and I had a sense that he was standing before me, holding me. As I close my eyes and think back to that moment, it's as if someone was wrapping their arms around me with the purest form of love I had ever known! It was a form of peace that washed over me from my head to my toes. In those brief minutes, all my pain and fears simply vanished and I heard the words, 'It's ok' being repeated. It was like the softest melody my ears had ever heard, and I felt nothing but pure love.

In that very moment, nurses came rushing into my room and began calling my name, shaking me back to reality. They informed me that AJ needed an emergency procedure; it was a matter of life or death! They handed me a piece of paper as they needed my signature for them to perform what they felt was going to save my son's life. But I already knew his life was saved.

I signed as quickly as I could and grabbed one nurse's hand as she gave the paper to the other nurse who went running down the hall. I told her, 'AJ is ok.' She replied, 'I pray you're right, Mrs. Martincic.' I asked her to take me to him so that I could kiss him one more time and tell him what I knew to be true. I grabbed the holy water that lay next to me; even though my son had been baptised earlier by the hospital priest, I needed to bless him myself. When I saw AJ, I leaned over to kiss him, and made the sign of the cross over him as I placed the holy water upon his head. I told my son that everything was ok and that God had said he could stay with me. I told AJ he didn't have to leave us and that I was going to be his mother. As I kissed him and told him how much he was loved, I just kept repeating the words I had heard from God: 'It will be ok, AJ.' And I knew in my heart it would.

When the sun hit my face, I gasped as I reached for the phone to call the NICU. The nurse who answered informed me that AJ was alive, and I thanked God over and over again for allowing our son to stay with us. AJ was still in a critical condition, but he was alive. I knew our son was going to overcome any issues he was facing and that he would be coming home with us. This experience was nothing other than a gift from God. To this day, I don't know why I received God's miracle, but I am grateful for the opportunity to be AJ's mother.

The next five days felt like a dream, but each day I would sit with my son and I would be amazed at what my eyes could see. This precious baby was so small, so fragile, and so sick, I didn't have the ability to comprehend all that was happening. I would go back and forth from my room to his, like a walking zombie, appearing lifeless but trying to function in society.

As I woke on my last day that I was able to stay in the hospital, I didn't have a clue that it was Mother's Day, until a sweet elderly woman came into my room with a handmade gift made by volunteers to wish me a very special Mother's Day. All I could think of was that my sweet little girls hadn't seen their mother in a week, and I felt terrible. It was too much to bear as I realized how scared they must have been with their mother in hospital and their baby brother fighting for his life. As I looked at the gift that was given to me, I burst into tears. It was Mother's Day, for God's sake, and it was Miranda's 6th birthday. And I wasn't with any of my babies! My world was a mess and I felt like I had failed them all.

As the nurses started the process of discharging me, I found myself unable to stop the tears from streaming down my face. As I sat before AJ, one nurse bent down and said, 'Please don't cry. We're going to take such great care of your baby, we promise.' She hugged me, and I melted in her arms and said, 'Thank you, but it's Mother's Day. How can I leave him when I haven't even held my baby yet?' She looked at me as though she felt every inch of my pain and said, 'You're not leaving this hospital until you hold your son.' I sobbed with relief and excitement that I could finally hold my beautiful baby, kiss his face, and whisper in his ears my unconditional love for him.

It took several doctors and several tests before they could place him in my arms, and as my body touched his I crumbled to pieces. I will never forget that moment as long as I live. It is one that changed me forever. The emotions my husband and I felt on that Mother's Day are ones we can't really discuss, but we knew we were being given a second chance. As I reluctantly handed AJ back to his doctors, I felt as if someone was ripping my heart out of my chest.

I was wheeled out of the hospital, and I remember feeling like someone had thrown me into another reality. Everything felt different and unrecognizable, and I knew my world was never going to be the same as it had been just five days before. As we drove closer to our home, I had to find the courage to put a smile on my face for my beautiful daughters, who were waiting with such excitement for their mother to come home. They needed me and I needed them, because their love is what had got me through those really dark days.

I assured them that AJ was doing well, that he would be home very soon, and they could hold their little brother as they were supposed to. We had been denied those very special and tender first days of bringing a baby into this world, but we were so grateful that our son, their brother, was still in our world.

We couldn't wait for the day that our AJ would come home so that we could bring an end to this turbulent time, but little did we know, this was just the beginning.

A message to my younger self...

If I could go back in time and speak to that scared young mother, I would tell her to trust in the power of the unseen and to have faith in her ability to overcome whatever she

115

is faced with. I would tell her to never give up on herself, because she is the girl who refuses to quit and so are you.

You're meant to live a life of love and prosperity filled with happiness, purpose and creation. You are the purest form of love, and must do and be love.

Nothing is a failure, nothing is a waste, it is a step and an adventure to get to the next chapter of your story. When I look back on all my successes and my failures, each was a divine gift needed for me to learn a greater lesson. What matters most is what you do with that lesson and how you expand because of it.

Think of your soul as being on a mission to acquire lessons. Learn from them, and allow them to teach you that your inner strength and intuition is your connection to God. The problem where most get caught is that they don't see the lesson that was meant to be learned. Many ignore the greater picture and do not understand how they were meant to grow from that, not just experience it. They end up spending a lifetime repeating similar experiences and falling victim to their circumstances. Some might even become depressed, turn to outside sources to find peace and happiness, or even destructive behaviour. They begin to make choices that make them feel good in that moment rather than what's best for them in the bigger picture of their life.

You are meant to live a life that is heart-led, soul-centred, and full of lessons that expand you. You are meant to tune into what sets your soul on fire and tap into the energy of your divine purpose. You are meant for greatness because you were made from greatness, and I was meant to teach you this. My purpose is to teach you the lessons I've learned so that you do not have to go through the struggles that I went through. My purpose is to heal your soul and make you aware that you are and will forever be connected to divine love.

I now feel that greatness is a gift that lies in your soul; your imagination is a place where you can live and create the experiences you want to have. When I look back, I realise this is exactly what I did to overcome and survive my experience. The change won't happen overnight, and you will not know all the details of how it will come together. Faith is the belief in the unseen, and this is about you never letting go of that gift, never quitting on your future and who you have yet to become. I can honestly say this is how I approach my life and all my experiences.

I am a strong, loving soul, who will never doubt her intuition. I am finding purpose in helping others to discover their divine connection.

I am The Girl Who Refused to Quit.

Dedication

For my family; thank you for always loving and supporting me on my journey.

About the Author

Larissa, who lives in Queens, New York, has been described as 'a spiritual soul powered by intuition to serve others'!

When she's not mentoring women or creating powerful soul charts, Larissa can often be found enjoying life with her wonderful husband, beautiful children, and adorable dogs!

She is a very proud Intuitive Numerologist, who has committed to her own journey of personal and spiritual alignment.

Larissa's mission is to impact, inspire, and breathe life into others, so they can experience love, growth, and joy. Her guidance is making a powerful difference in the world, one connection at a time, helping others to discover their destiny.

Contact

www.larissamartincic.com
hello@larissamartincic.com
Facebook/ LarissaMartincic
Facebook/ GoddessGiving
Instagram @GoddessGiving

Addicted to Love
Alexandra Prince

I stood shaking at the edge of the 46th floor balcony of my luxury apartment in Dubai Marina. I was ready to jump. I was ready to end it all. With my mobile phone in my trembling hand, I called my parents to say a final goodbye. 'I can't, Dad, I can't live any more. I don't want to live. Help me jump, Dad. Please, Dad. If you love me, help me jump.'

My cries were deep. The pain cut so badly, so excruciatingly deep that my soul no longer knew how to fight. I was once again back at square one. Abandoned, lost, heartbroken, and in excruciating pain from the withdrawal symptoms of my most recent, intensely passionate relationship falling apart. Anxiety and shame consuming every part of my fearful being, I'd finally had enough.

Without the high of love, I'd rather be dead. That's what I thought.

I had tried, but I couldn't battle my way out of this one. Not this time. Not again. I could hear my dad trying to stay calm on the other end of the line. He was thousands of miles away, but in that phone call we made a pact that if I still felt the same way when I got back to the UK, then

119

I was free to do as I wished. But for now, I would go back to the only place I knew as home. My parents' place. The small, three bed, semi-detached home I'd grown up in as a child on the outskirts of London.

My brother was home that day from Norfolk, and was standing close to the phone alongside my Mum and Dad. It was coming up to Christmas 2010, just under two years since I'd first arrived in Dubai. And Alexandra, also known by the voices in my head as 'used goods, broken, dirty, and unwanted', was ready to die. I'd finally been defeated by the nasty names and the dark voices that were out to finish me. Depression and rejection had won the battle, and like so many other times in those darker days, I would repeatedly say to myself, 'I can't take any more of this pain. Please God. I can't do this any more.'

Like so many little girls, for years I'd fallen prisoner to the fairytale delusion of forever searching for my perfect prince, only to be traumatised by the agony of deceit time and time again. The truth was I would never find true happiness whilst I was unknowingly repeating a pattern of what I later learned to understand as 'love addiction'. I was hooked on love like a drug addict hooked on heroin, constantly searching for the euphoric high of a new relationship, only to be devastated when it crashed.

I didn't even know what real love felt like, because for as long as I can remember I associated love as being an intense high and a painful crash. The pleasure followed by pain had become an addiction. I'd destroy perfectly healthy relationships because I needed that fix of a high then a low; or I'd choose to chase dysfunctional, emotionally unavailable men, because I'd thrive from the highs and the lows of what a relationship like that could offer me. The make-up sex, the instability, the addiction to pain and pleasure, had been what I'd known for pretty much most of my adult life. It came with the territory of seeking danger, bad boys, and sleeping with men who predominately had come from very troubled childhoods.

I felt so worthy when I was rescuing someone else from their own difficult past, because it meant I could deflect the responsibility of facing my own insecurities and shadow self. But I would feel equally worthless when the relationship would dramatically end, usually because we were both in some way trying to gain some kind of manipulation or control over one another. It was like a challenge to see if I could actually get a damaged man to become my perfect prince. But essentially, that was never going to happen.

As a daughter from humble beginnings, born into a loving middle-class family, I still wonder how by just 19 years old I'd found myself inside the circles of the world's wealthiest elite. I was just a normal girl who attended an average school. I got my first part-time job at my local football ground, aged 15 years old, and I remember telling my dad that one day I would become the girlfriend of an international football star. Like many of the dreams I'd proclaimed to my father as a child, I *did* become the girlfriend of an international football star. I also walked the red carpet and partied on luxury yachts, just as I had promised I would do. But with this extravagant and sometimes shallow lifestyle, came a lifelong battle of chasing my self-worth, which ultimately led to me seeking dysfunctional and co-dependent relationships.

It was during my first few months of working at a top West End nightclub that I was headhunted by a short and rather elf-like looking man; let's call him John. He invited me to be a part of a new girl band, and told me that he thought I had what it took to be the next Spice Girl. Of course, like any other typical fame-hungry teenager who had grown up dreaming of becoming a Spice Girl, this was like winning the lottery. The year was 1999, and in typical Leo style, I was adamant that I was born to live a lifestyle like the rich and famous. John was my first introduction into this new world, and as time went on, I would regularly meet with him to go to a recording studio in Essex. He told me I should be very grateful that he had chosen me to be his next project and that thousands of girls would do anything to be in my position. Each time we met it, became apparent that he wanted a lot more than just a singing and dancing rehearsal.

I don't recall much about the owner of the mansion in Essex where I went with John to record my vocals, but once we arrived we would head down to the basement studio within this huge and luxurious mansion, where there were lots of awards on the walls, gold vinyls, and black and white pictures of famous musicians from the 70s and 80s. The house was clearly a great set-up to impress young girls like me, and an outgoing VIP nightclub hostess was the perfect candidate for John to seduce. I knew it was wrong, but he had the key to my dreams and, as a recently turned 19-year-old, I really didn't know how to handle this.

If you're reading this now and know me personally, then you may be thinking, *I didn't know you could sing, Alexandra!* Or that I'd be as naive as to give this guy what he wanted. Well, you're right. I wasn't the best singer, but with an attractive figure, long brown wavy hair, dimples in my cheeks, and a killer smile, I certainly looked the part – and for a good few months John continued to groom me. He bought me clothes, a car, jewellery; all as a part of my supposed record deal. He made me feel like a star. I wasn't like all my other friends who had to suffer the dreary commute and a 9 to 5 office job. So when push came to shove, I naively felt that I owed him for giving me the keys to a lifestyle most could only dream of.

I know writing this now it sounds ludicrous. Why had I accepted those gifts? Why had I allowed him to take advantage? Was this taking advantage, or did I ask for it? After all, I was 19 years old and a consenting adult. Well, let me tell you this right now. I was a vulnerable young woman desperate for validation, and as a nearly 40-year-old woman, I now understand I was not to blame. I was a young, impressionable woman falling deeper and deeper into the allure of a lifestyle and career that made me feel like I was finally worth something. I didn't have the courage or maturity to back out of his demands, so instead I prayed that one day soon he would come good and I would forget about what I'd actually done for my so-called music career.

Of course, in the end nothing did come of my elusive recording deal. I look back now and can clearly see that this degrading experience was just the beginning of me no longer loving or respecting myself, which resulted in me developing damaging traits of co-dependency. I became accustomed to using my looks as a bargaining tool to get what I wanted, and this is the pattern of how my life played out for a very long time. It became the norm for me to manipulate and use my sexuality to get something in return. But afterwards, I would feel worthless, ashamed, and guilty. I'd often find myself being seduced by older men who would offer me all sorts of lavish gifts and promises of success, and I'd follow through because I didn't realise just how much I was hurting myself. They say that nothing in this life comes for free, and I can certainly say that I feel I paid the price.

At 24, and for three beautiful years, I got together with a good man – a humble, kind, and honourable man with a decent job, a wonderful family, and honest values. I loved nothing more than to be at home in my onesie with him, simply cuddling on the sofa or going to the local pub with his family. We had some of the best years of my life, doing the most normal and what may seem mundane of things. But over time I found myself unconsciously doing everything in my power to destroy him until he left me, and I went back to chasing the high of a wealthy, destructive lifestyle. I'd already done this once before with another really nice and honourable man. It was as if I refused to allow myself the happiness of a simple, pain-free relationship. I craved drama!

To mask the confusion of what my soul was actually craving and what my ego would destroy, I found solace in VIP parties, alcohol, and sometimes drugs. In my later twenties, I began mixing with some of the wealthiest and most influential men on the planet. Football players, businessmen, rap artists, you name it. By aged 30, I'd moved to Dubai and flown in private jets a multitude of times. In fact, I was even headhunted by a billionaire business tycoon to become his private flight attendant. I frequented 6-star Arabian hotels, tanned on 180-foot royal yachts, and travelled to numerous countries – all whilst hanging out with men worth multiple millions. I know it all sounds like an amazing lifestyle, but the truth was I had never been so depressed. My soul was empty. I'd left two beautiful, honest relationships and instead found myself in a world where I felt like nothing more than a disposable party piece.

This wasn't where I wanted to be.

I wanted to be in a beautiful, loving, soulful relationship with a man who worshipped me, and where I could express my truth. Why did I keep destroying things to chase an illusion of fame and fortune? The truth was that I didn't even really care about money or fame. I just wanted to be loved and to feel safe. But how would I ever achieve that when I kept destroying any chance of true happiness?

I felt like I'd spent my entire life sabotaging myself, my happiness, and my success.

It didn't matter that I'd managed to achieve a top-class fashion degree from the prestigious London College of Fashion, or that I had the ability to achieve most things I put my mind to. For as long as I can remember, I never believed I was good enough or that I deserved true love and success.

At one point in my early thirties, from the outside looking in I appeared to have it all. I met a handsome, older, wealthy partner and I travelled the world with him. We would go to Dubai, New York, Saint Tropez, Rome, Paris, Geneva, you name it, skiing in Europe's finest resorts, and dining in the best Michelin star restaurants in the world. But looks can be deceiving. Behind this jet-set life was an emotionally void, controlling man who made me feel like shit. He didn't meet any of my emotional needs and, despite the lavish lifestyle, I found myself slipping further and further into depression.

It was as if there were two sides to me. On the one side was a beautiful, energetic, and bubbly woman who lit up the world with her infectious energy, tenacious ambition, and killer smile. But on the other side was a deeply confused woman, lost and insecure, who was lonely, emotionally drained, and searching for love in all the wrong places. There I was pretending that Alexandra was living her best life, when in actual fact I was living a lonely existence in a relationship where I felt like nothing more than a trophy mistress. He, of course, told me that he was separated, but as time went on it became obvious that I was not the only woman in his life. Yet again, I felt betrayed and worthless.

Albert Einstein proclaimed that the definition of insanity is doing the same thing again and again and expecting a different result. Well, this had become my life. A different man but the same patterns of dishonesty and abuse. I refused to settle for a nice guy and instead tortured myself with trying to win over the affection of men who were essentially toxic.

After 15 years of repeating these relationship patterns, I've since been on a journey of spiritual self-discovery and healing. But I want to be honest with you and say that still, to this day, I struggle hugely with my self-worth and my addiction to unhealthy patterns in love.

I have periods where I feel completely empowered and think I'm finally on the full road to recovery, but even as a qualified life coach and healer, I am still very much on my own transformational journey. As a life coach, I used to feel embarrassed to admit to people that I still feel scared and lost sometimes. But I now realise that my authenticity is one of my greatest strengths. Because in so many ways I've totally transformed my life, but in other ways I know I still have a massive battle ahead of me.

More recently, I found myself suffering a miscarriage in a relationship that I thought was going to be my happy-ever-after. In this relationship, things seemed so different. I'd done so much work on self-love that I didn't think I'd ever attract anyone into my life that was remotely unstable. He was kind, soft, loving, and attentive, but it sadly turned out that my partner was battling a secret addiction. This meant I had to part ways with him whilst I was pregnant, and I believe the stress brought on the miscarriage. It's sometimes in moments like this where I no longer want to be the girl who refused to quit. In fact, I want to quit and give up and wallow in my grief and humiliation, but I know that God has other plans for me. Because I now understand that it is only through our greatest lessons that I believe we can truly help to serve and heal others. He only gives the toughest lessons to the strongest of characters. He only gives us what he knows we can handle.

It was five years ago that I went from living in mansions and hanging out on yachts to finding myself six-foot under, heartbroken, and knowing I had to truly heal my life. For the five years since, I have been on a radical journey of self-love and spiritual self-discovery, including spending a year in Thailand on my own journey of '*Eat Pray Love*'! I've called this journey 'My Beautiful Ugly Awakening' and it is now something I coach and teach to other women as I support and guide them through their own process of awakening and spiritual healing.

A beautiful yet ugly awakening is where we bring our greatest darkness to the light, so we can surrender to the truth of our journey and our higher power. A bit like the 12 steps in Alcoholics Anonymous, the first step is to admit we are powerless to our addictions but there is a power greater than us that if we choose to access, can help us heal.

The truth is that our souls are worth more than giving into a life of unhealthy patterns and lack of self-worth, and through healing ourselves we also help to heal our family lineage.

I've learned how to be kinder to myself, how to forgive myself and fall in love with me, even when the chips are down. I also know how to spot the red flags sooner, which is why I had the courage to exit my last relationship despite being pregnant at the time and terrified of being alone. The truth is there is nothing outside of myself that can fill me up like unconditional self-love and self-respect, and despite the grief of my miscarriage, I know that I am deserving of a healthy relationship and a life free from addiction, pain, and conflict.

Over the past few years as a transformational life coach, I have found myself speaking across the world including to an audience of thousands in the capital of the United States in Washington D.C. I've taught self-love and mindset workshops around the world, and hosted a workshop in my dream destination of Bali, Indonesia. This never would have happened if I hadn't decided to begin doing the work to love and heal myself, although I openly admit that I am still a work in progress.

I believe owning and sharing all of my story has been one of the most transformational and fundamental parts of my healing journey. We think the safe or easy option is to hide our past regrets and experiences; those parts of ourselves that we are deeply ashamed of. But I've since found that by claiming all of my truth, I've enabled myself to heal and rise into my greatest spiritual calling.

I now have a mission to speak up and help educate young women on love addiction, as well as the power of self-love and forgiveness. To truly love and respect ourselves is the most powerful gift we can give ourselves, and there is nobody in this world who can tell you that you are not enough.

My past experience, along with my shame, is now dead and buried. But I now have a duty to continue my healing. I believe we can only take our clients as far as we have taken ourselves, but what I want you to know is that to teach and empower, you only need be one step ahead of those who need your help. That is why I call myself the girl who refused to quit, because I don't claim to be perfect, but I claim to be the woman who uses my truth and authentic nature to support you with the lessons I have already accomplished.

We are all on a lifelong journey of graduating from the lessons we asked to come here to learn. As spiritual beings, we are having a human experience which includes feeling what it's like to suffer. So, don't be so hard on yourself when pain strikes, and remember that together we are all simply the girls who refused to quit.

A message to my younger self...

If I could go back in time and speak to my younger self, I'd want her to know that time and knowledge really are the greatest healers. Our goal is not simply to live an incredible, pain-free life, but to learn how to overcome the challenges and lessons that we have asked to come here to learn in order to reach a greater level of enlightenment.

I wished I had known that my life would be filled with many romantic relationships, and that until I truly did the work to heal myself, I would keep attracting the same suffering.

Being able to survive everything I went through has shown me that I am the girl who refused to quit. That I will not allow my challenges to harden me, but I will do my best to continue on my healing path so I can truly soften and conquer my addictions once and for all.

It has taught me that I embrace my truth and love, and claim all of who I was and all who I have become. So, I tell you this story today to encourage you to claim all of you. There is nothing about your past that has the right to define who you are today. I am writing this chapter with my head held high and my shame well and truly in the past, because the only way to set the light free within me was to break down the walls that were keeping it hidden. It was time to stop searching for something outside of me, and it was time to trust that I had the power within me all along to be the best and highest version of me. Because the truth is that I am perfect, and I am whole. I always was and I always will be. And so are you.

I now feel I can look and understand that every single

part of my journey has been a beautiful blessing that has led me towards a deeper spiritual mission. A mission in which I have now awakened to what I understand to be my 'calling'. In the Bible (Matthew 22:14), Matthew says, '...for many are called, but few are chosen'. What I believe he means by this is that many are called but few have the courage to answer. Few are brave enough to move beyond the judgment, the guilt, and the shame of the roads they travelled in order to awaken to the light. This chapter is my call to you. A call to be brave and to own your truth and your suffering, no matter what, so that you can move beyond the darkness and into the light of a future that you were always meant to live.

If you are going through a similar time right now, I want you to understand that time heals everything, and that awareness is the first key to change.

I am whole. I am complete. I am enough.

I am The Girl Who Refused to Quit.

Dedication

For all the brave women who choose to rise again, no matter what.

About the Author

Alexandra Prince is a Transformational Life Coach, Certified Theta Healer, and Motivational Speaker, who helps women to reconnect with their divine truth. Her mission is to empower you to heal and rise, through learning how to tap into a greater spiritual power. Her area of expertise is supporting those who are overcoming separation and heartbreak to find strength in a new beginning. She is deeply committed to helping you reclaim your confidence and personal power, so you can attract everything you desire in your life and business. She resides in London, and is a proud dog mama to her French Bulldog Buster Prince!

Contact

www.alexandraprince.co
hello@alexandraprince.co
Facebook/@alexandraprinceco
Instagram/ @alexandraprinceco
Alexandra will be publishing her first book in 2020.

The Shadows of You
Lisa Martin

The scream ripped through me as I lay in the inky darkness of that small bedroom, feeling like I had experienced an electric shock, half wanting to stay asleep, but feeling like I should be awake, the dream waking me from my slumber. With a whimper, I lay there in the darkness of which I was totally petrified.

I tried to snuggle deeper into my cosy waffle eiderdown, my back sticking to my sweaty flannelette sheets. I lay there, trying not to make a sound, too scared to look to see any movements hidden within the shadows. But needing to check on my baby brother who shared my room, with frightened eyes I scanned the room to see his small body gently sleeping. As my eyes adjusted to the darkness, I heard it again, only this time louder!

Another scream ripped through the blackness and tore my little soul in two. For this was no dream; it was a nightmare that was about to become all too real for me. I knew no matter how scared I was feeling, I had to go and try to stop him.

As I crept down the stairs with my little legs shaking, I shivered from head to toe, my torn nightie not quite reaching my knees. Each step seemed to take an age, my hand on the wall for support as I chewed on my bottom lip, my heart beating wildly in my chest. I finally reached the bottom step with my tiny hand holding tightly onto the bannister rail.

The door was open a tiny crack and I stood trying to peek through with one eye shut to see better, trying to see her, to check if she was ok. I heard the thud, so loud it vibrated through the floor under my bare feet. It was then that I pushed the door silently all the way open. The sight that hit me had me shaking so much that I was almost dancing on the spot. The wreckage before me I can't fully describe, even now all these years later: the smashed records strewn all over the carpet; the chair tipped over, with a smashed cup by its side; books pulled from the shelves with their pages flapping open.

It was then I saw her, lying with her head on the marble hearth. A trickle of blood was running from her skin. He had one hand on her throat, the other hand holding onto her narrow wrist, as he gripped her hand. There are some words no child should ever have to hear being spoken, never mind witnessing the horrific scene before me, but I did! I finally found my voice, and shouted, 'Please stop hurting my mum! Please stop! You're killing her!'

It was only when I launched myself into the room, my hands tearing at his, screaming to let my mummy go, that he realized he had company. And he let my crying, battered, and bruised mum go, with a kiss to her lips, saying to me, 'Sweetheart, we were only playing.' And with that, I ran back up the stairs and hid under those sweaty bedcovers, shaking and shivering, silent tears streaming from my eyes, not wanting the morning to arrive.

He had always had a short temper. I remember him often snapping at me and my baby brother. Sometimes it was for no reason other than he wanted a cigarette, or he would say tea wasn't cooked properly so he couldn't eat it. Even though it was lovingly prepared and ready when he got in through the door, and the table always set with her finest china.

He had high expectations of us as a family. The house always had to be immaculate, nothing out of place. My brother and I always had to be dressed in our Sunday best, our shoes shining like mirrors. But nothing ever seemed good enough, and we were often told we had to be good or we'd see the buckle of his belt, the back of his hand, or he'd tell us that naughty children get taken away.

He was always shouting at Mum, telling her she looked a mess and he was disgusted at her, even though he insisted she always wore a dress. There was one particular dress I loved on her – it was long and red, and she looked beautiful in it. There was a photograph of her wearing it in our house. They say a picture paints a thousand words, and even though she was smiling, if you looked closely enough you could see the sadness in her eyes. I loved seeing my mum look all pretty, her nails painted; her hair and makeup were never out of place.

When the shouting got too bad, my mum would usher me and my brother up to the room we shared, and she would tell us not to come out until she said it was ok. I would create stories to stop my baby brother from crying and hold him until his sobs subsided.

As far back as I can remember, he was a man who rarely smiled. A man who controlled us with words, actions, and fists. But when he did smile at us, gave us praise, or we had a day out as a family, it was as if the dark clouds had lifted and the world became a brighter place. Like the time he took us around the block in his shiny new car, the sun shining so hot on the bonnet you could fry an egg on it. He didn't stop smiling and laughing with us! I imagined I was a princess and he was my prince taking me for a ride in his carriage.

Or the time we went to Mother Shipton's cave in Yorkshire. I wore my favourite red coat, and my long hair was curly from all the pipe cleaners my mum had spent hours putting in the night before so that I would look pretty for him, and so that he would be proud of me. I don't remember the finer details of that day, just that it was a day where we laughed and he was smiling… that is until suddenly, in the car on the way home, his mood turned dark, like a light being switched off, plunging us all into darkness, and we were left wondering what on earth we had done wrong now!

My lips trembled with unshed tears as he snatched hold of Mum's wrist. She tried to hide the fear in her eyes with a smile on her face, telling us it was ok, everything was ok. Of course, I knew in my heart it wouldn't be, as he started shouting at her. Clinging onto each other's hands, my finger stroked my brother's thumb to reassure him that the shouting would soon stop. I tried to take his mind of it by playing a game of I-spy, where we had to spot a certain coloured car as it drove past us.

I was relieved when the car finally pulled to stop on our street. But he jumped out, his blue eyes had turned a darker shade like a stormy sea – swirling greys, greens and flashes of blue. He pulled Mum roughly from her seat, saying through gritted teeth, 'Out!'

Mum walked as fast as she could to the front door, before turning to me and saying to me, 'You and your brother go to Aunty L's, I'll come and get you in a little while.' Aunty L was my mum's best friend who lived next door-but-one to us in our small row of terraced houses. The front of the houses faced our local woods, where we would spend hours exploring, pretending to be pirates and princesses, or looking for bugs and picking bluebells.

I knocked on the bright red door of Aunty L's house. She let us in, no questions asked, gave us a hug and sent us into the back garden to play with her kids. By the time we had had our tea, it was getting dark and I asked when Mum would be coming for us. I was tired and my brother was scared, not knowing what was going on. At that moment, Mum walked through the door, her lip swollen. There was a red mark on her face, her eyes red-ringed as though she had been crying, and one eye looking darker than the other.

'Right, you lot, time for bed. Go on upstairs, you can all top and tail. Keep the noise down and be good. I'll be up to tuck you all in in a minute. I'm just going to make your mum a cup of tea,' Aunty L said.

The last thing I remember that night is making sure my brother was washed and tucked into bed, whilst Aunty L's daughter snuggled into me and told me, 'Don't worry, I'm your friend forever.' She held my hand while I cried myself to sleep.

Life returned to normal for a little while, even if mum was quieter than usual. He was even smiling, but that made me wary. Even at such a young age, I seemed to sense it was the calm before the storm. My days should have been carefree, and mostly they were. We had a close family, with my mum's parents, brothers, and sisters nearby. We lived in a rough part of town that had a real sense of community where we made the best of what we had. We all knew each other, and the other parents didn't mind watching the kids as we played in the street.

None of our families had much in the way of money, but we had oodles of tough love, a dry home, and clean clothes. In fact, Mum used to make a lot of mine and I had some really weird but wonderful dresses. My nan knitted for everyone, so we were never short of knitted cardigans, jumpers, balaclavas, or knee-high knitted socks for when one of us had chilblains.

In those carefree early days in the community, we were surrounded by friends and neighbours. Our days were spent in the shadow of love under the watchful eyes of my guardian angels, my North and my South – the two people, apart from my mum, who taught me right from wrong. The ones who gave me a voice from an early age, and the freedom to use it.

My beloved Nan and Granddad were the very best grandparents any child could ever wish for. Gone now, but you will never be forgotten – you, and your words and your guidance live inside my heart always.

Dad, I remember the day you left us, no words, no hugs, and no goodbyes. You walked out the door, up the front path, never once looking back. I actually felt relieved, even a little bit lucky – no more shouting, no more hurting, or so I thought. How wrong was I? When I realised he was gone for good, I had some pretty confusing and overwhelming emotions: Why am I not good enough? Why am I not worth loving? Why does he not like me? Why does he hate us? And what did we do wrong?

A few years later when I found out that my dad and his new wife were having a baby – their first child together – it smacked me hard in the face. It brought up all the feelings of why we, his first family, were not good enough. Why were we not enough for him? Why were we unwanted? Seeing him excited to love and want a new child, when he seemingly didn't want the two children he already had, really hurt. I ran and ran from the hurt in my heart. I ranted, I cried, I called him every name I could think of and then some. For a little girl with no real knowledge of the words to use, let me tell you, I'm sure I used words I didn't even know what they meant. I knew it was complicated and it was shit, but it was my new reality.

All I knew was that my dad had a new family and I no longer knew where my brother and I would fit in. No-one told me how it would be, how I would feel, or how to deal with the rawness of his loss. I felt helpless in my grief of wanting him back, but not wanting the shouting or the hurt any more.

I grew up always feeling the odd one out, and would compare myself to the kids who had both a mum and dad that loved and protected them. I admit I felt jealous, sad, angry, and unhappy. I felt like I was different, and that everyone was laughing at the bucked-teeth girl because her father had left her. I didn't know how to change that fact. Like it or not, they all had a mum and a dad… and I didn't… and it hurt. I did my best to fit in, but let me tell you it's exhausting, and leaves you feeling shite about yourself 24/7, even when you don't want it to be like that.

The sadness, the feeling scared, the feeling ashamed, the guilt, the anger, and the sheer shitty loneliness, is by far the hardest part to deal with. It takes you by the throat and hangs you out to dry.

The aftermath of a life lived with violence, love, and loss, leaves you shattered by the force of your emotions. I wasn't prepared for how much losing you would hurt. The bone-wracking sobs I'd cry, alone in my room, so I wouldn't upset Mum. All the while telling myself you weren't worth it; you didn't love me anyway; and that I could be strong. Until I couldn't, then I'd cry some more. You were supposed to protect me, support me, and guide me through life.

But you didn't, and I still often wonder why? When I'd been raped and beaten, were you there with an arm to hold me? Did you even care? When I was hurting at the loss of you, did you think of us? The kids you left behind.

Do I miss you? How can I miss what I never had? You gave me nothing to miss. I have already cried enough tears for what will never be, for what I've never had, for the hope that I still hold dear in my heart and the answers only you can give me.

But here's the truth, and the cruellest twist of all: I've learned that you never stop wanting things to be different. I'm still hoping for that little glint of light, a crack in the shadows. The hope that one day you might give me the words I have always longed to hear. The words 'I love you. I missed you. I didn't give up on you or your brother.'

So how the hell do you heal from the heartbreak and pain? How do you soothe the hurting child that beats within your soul? I never realized until recently that subconsciously, and over my shoulder, I'd been thinking

I'd seen him in the corners, or in shadowed doorways. I'd notice a grey-haired man with piercing blue eyes, and my heart would skip a beat, and I'd think, *There he is, that's my dad*.

You always think throughout life, *Is this the year I'll get a birthday card?* or *Is this the year he will call me, or he will come to visit me?* But then it never happens, or when you do see him at family events, he will hug you. But no hug is ever given, no real acknowledgement of what your meant to mean to each other, and you think, *Oh well, maybe next year*. And you begin searching the crowds in your mind once again for a glimpse, a smile, a hug... or even a punch. For when you've lived through a life tinged with violence, hurt, and abandonment, it lives in your heart forever. But yet you keep hoping for the one last chance with your absent dad, where he would see he was wrong, and he would reach out and be the dad you wanted – the protector, the rock, the hero. I always wished for that, and it makes me feel sad that this was the truth in my life. For so long, I had this dead weight in my tummy, constantly churning.

I have a wonderful, amazing stepdad, who has helped to guide me through the many curveballs in my life, who was and has been there for me when I needed a shoulder to cry on, when I needed a helping hand, when I needed lifting up because my burdens were too heavy to carry alone. The man who has loved and looked after my mum for the last 43-plus years, the man I call Dad because he has earned that title over and over again. I love him like a daughter should, in all the ways it matters, because to me, he is my dad.

But yet, the loss of you, Dad – the one who gave me life – feels heavy, and oh so deep. I wonder, will I have time to get the answers I am yearning for, or will the end of you come with no hope, and only sadness for a life left without you? That this is just the way it was meant to be. A father gone, but not forgotten. A weight on my shoulders, with those damn questions still left on my lips and that heaviness in my heart.

Every day I ask, will I be devastated when my dad finally dies? Of course I will. I loved him, despite it all.

A message to my younger self...

If I could go back and speak to my younger self, I would tell her you were not bad. You were good enough. You didn't deserve the pain; the pain you carried alone. It was ok to believe in those fairytales' goodness, happiness, and love. That despite it all, you were the bravest girl I knew, the girl who always gave the best of herself and saw only the best in others.

Going through and growing through everything I have, has taught me that I am stronger than I think and that I am totally worthy of love. I now feel strong, I have faith in myself and in my own abilities as a mum, a partner, and a businesswoman.

And as I look back on my life, I wonder if this was how it was always meant to be. Was I given this journey to understand it, was this always my purpose? To help others, so they don't lie awake in the darkness crying silent tears and asking themselves, 'Why me?' Wishing there was just one person out there who would understand.

If you are going through a similar situation, I want you

to know that you can't know what you don't know! I want you to know I'm so proud of you for getting through the hurt and the heartache. I'm so proud of you that you have done whatever you needed to do to survive.

I want you to know, you are not worthless. You are good enough. You didn't do anything wrong.

We are not the victims in our story. We are the survivors. Our past may have shaped us, but it does not define us. We can rewrite our story.

I am unstoppable.

I am The Girl Who Refused to Quit.

Dedication

This chapter is dedicated to all who grew up without the love and support they needed; to the ones who wondered why they weren't enough.

The ones who struggled to love themselves.

To those whose heart hung onto a tiny silver thread of hope for a better tomorrow.

Together, we can rewrite our stories.

About the Author

Lisa Martin, who lives in East Yorkshire, has been described as a caring, inspiring person, who is powered by grit, grace, and soul.

She has gone through, and grown through, so many

curveballs in life with tears and a smile, determined not to be broken, and uncovering her purpose.

When she is not coaching clients, giving a talk or workshop, Lisa can be found being creative, or writing her life story in the hope of empowering others to know they are not alone.

She is a passionate advocate for women who have lived with abuse of any kind, of guiding you from trauma and heartbreak, from lost and overwhelm to being found.

Contact

www.lisamartindesigns.com
www.instagram.com/lisamartindesigns
https://www.facebook.com/pages/Lisa Martin Designs
https://www.facebook.com/groups/soulpowerqueen
https://linkedin.com/Lisa Martin
Lisa will be publishing her first book in 2020.

A Mother's Love

Jacqueline E Rogerson

No mother should ever have to hear the words 'I'm so sorry, but there's no sign of your child's heart beating'.

I was just 20 years old, and my whole world collapsed in that moment. Nothing could ever be the same again. He was my second child – the first baby I had planned, dreamed about, and yearned for. How could this be happening? I was so excited, ready for his arrival, and after nine months and one week of a relatively uneventful pregnancy, he was gone… 'just' like that. On that dark January day in 1996, my whole life changed forever. I sat in shock on that hospital bed, looking at the faces in the room, who were all looking at the screen in disbelief. There was no heartbeat to be heard and there was no sign of movement from my huge pregnant belly. A thousand questions whirred around in my head, the big 'WHY' shouting louder than all the rest. Why was I allowed to get this far in my pregnancy with no indication of anything being wrong? There must be something wrong with the baby, surely, it can't have just died? Why has this happened? How have I had such an active bump for nine months and a week, for it all just to stop now?

Of course, at that stage, no-one had the answers. We would surely find out later when they got the baby out. I didn't understand, couldn't pretend to grasp what was going on, because I was in shock. I had expected to go into labour, maybe a couple of days late, but wait a minute… what would happen now? Surely everything would just stop? I couldn't possibly have to give birth still, what would be the point? The world couldn't be so cruel as to expect me to have to go through any more pain? In a situation like that, it doesn't matter how many times you ask the medical profession right in front of you why, they don't have the answers. In fact, they seemed to be as stunned as us, asking what was the baby's due date again?

We were taken into a side room. It was quiet, and just a bit further away from the sound of newborn baby cries and just a bit further away from more heavily pregnant women who didn't look a lot different to me on the outside. Would we like a cup of tea? WE HAVE JUST BEEN TOLD OUR BABY'S DIED AND A CUP OF TEA IS SUPPOSED TO HELP?

Do we need to phone anyone? What were we supposed to say? As it was, both our families lived 160 miles away. Mum was expecting a call in the middle of the night, but not one like this. How could I tell her? What would I say? Obviously, I did; I had to. 'Are you ok? Have you had the baby?' There were a lot of confused questions and a lot of tears. Do I need her to let people know? I was in such shock that I just answered that we'd be home soon, and I'd call her later. That wasn't going to be enough. What mum would just sit waiting for more news after being told something like that over the phone at 3am? Her baby had now lost a baby, and she had lost a grandchild, too. It was all wrong; the natural order of things had been completely turned on its head.

The labour was mercifully short at just over four hours. I was shit scared of what was going to happen, and as I pushed him out, he just sort of 'fell' out. The room was truly, deathly silent. Except for the sound of our sobbing, and I am sure if you listened really carefully you could hear the sound of our hearts breaking.

We called him Jay. He weighed 8lbs 5oz, and was 58cms long, with all his fingers and toes – they were very long, too. I would say he was perfect, but of course had he been alive that would be more truthful.

He was the baby brother to our firstborn, Kieran, who I had given birth to at the tender age of just 16, when my introduction to the grown-up world of motherhood began.

Before Jay had even been born, we were asked if we wanted them to take him away and do the necessary (I still can't bear to think about that) post-mortem, to find out what the probable cause of death was. And had we started considering whether we would want him to be buried or cremated? What! We had never met our beautiful boy and now we had to think the unthinkable. Being a mum has come with more than its fair share of trials, but even having endured many episodes of stressful situations, unexpected outcomes, and difficult decisions, this was by far the worst.

As we walked silently away from the delivery suite, I was hesitant. It felt wrong, somehow, and I couldn't put my finger on it. Because, of course, I didn't want to leave him there, all alone in that side room with a big 'Do Not Enter' sign on the door. Everything was completely against the natural order of things. It didn't feel real. I wanted my baby back. How could I walk out of the door knowing that I'd never hold him again?

'Onward and Upward,' my gran said to me at his graveside on the darkest day, as we buried Jay in the cemetery, surrounded by our family and a handful of close friends.

At the time, I remember reading a SANDS (Stillbirth and Neonatal Death Society) book, called 'When a Baby Dies'. There was an account by a mum who became physically very unwell some 18 months after her child died, and she said she felt it was because she never allowed herself to grieve. Well, I wasn't going to let that happen to me. I was too young to write myself off now. I would grieve, I would do all the things I felt I needed to cope, to go through the emotions, to feel every possible pain there was, and embrace any opportunity no matter how painful it seemed at the time, all in the name of 'recovery'. I would listen to songs which had some significance over and over again and cry my eyes out. Often, it helped me feel closer to him for a time, but I am sure it helped me to heal, too. Eventually the time came when I had to look at a pregnant woman, or a new baby. Just remember, he/she isn't my baby – of course, all other babies were not as beautiful or perfect as mine! But that just made it hurt even more. All the babies born to mums at nursery at the time were boys, too.

In September 1996, I lost another baby at almost 11 weeks of pregnancy and started to feel as though perhaps I was only meant to ever have the one surviving child. I do not say that lightly; I know that so many couples are not even gifted with that, but for a very long time I truly felt that my heart would never be able to give all the love I had bottled up when Jay was tragically taken from us. I now understand that is because when you have all this love to give a child who can't be with you, you keep some in reserve somehow, because it belongs to them and it stays with you always.

December 1997

I braved it. We endured eight-and-a-half months of the unknown, but this time we truly understood there were no guarantees. Every waking morning came with the question, 'Is the baby still moving?' We had been loaned a portable sonograph by the midwife (she had been with us through everything), I had counselling, attended self-help group meetings every week without fail, and somehow, I managed to scrape through another pregnancy. To say it was stressful is an understatement, although not the biggest understatement of my life (that being the word 'awful', when used to describe the loss of a child – believe me, there is no word in the English language hideous enough to describe it). I was still grieving for Jay and that in itself was exhausting, yet somehow, I muddled through towards the light at the end of a dark and often lonely tunnel.

Our families and friends did everything they could to support us, but we had experienced the kind of loss none of them seemed able to relate to; they desperately wanted us to feel 'better'. What was that again? It was cushioned by writing about my feelings in a journal and visiting self-help groups. That saved me; that and the network of bereaved mums I had found my way to – the club no-one wants to belong to. These women were the only ones who truly understood my pain.

We cried tears of joy when they announced again…

It's a boy! This time, after a little medical intervention, early induction, and lots of scans and reassurance (no-one made us any promises, but it couldn't possibly happen again… could it?), he really was kicking and screaming his way into the world. And after a few days of trying to find the perfect name to fit, we called him Sam. He certainly made his presence felt, particularly because he didn't sleep through the night for a very long time. It's his way of letting us know he's here, I would say!

The relief that comes with something like that is impossible to describe. Thankful we got him out in time, because who knows why his brother died. Relieved, and sad; perhaps he would never have been conceived if Jay had made it. Kieran now had two younger brothers, but Sam would only ever know what we told him about his 'other' brother. And, of course, we would. Yet somehow you still don't feel complete (because you know deep down you never will), and that makes you feel bad too. The guilt for feeling happy is the hardest one to bear; it's as if you have forgotten about the saddest thing in your world, just for a moment. Of course, that's not true at all.

For a time, life muddled along. Jay had become part of our lives in his way and I would often see signs that he was around, like ladybirds showing up in the most curious of places; they were always at his graveside. I sort of got on with my life, the best way I knew how. I worked voluntarily for SANDS, giving something back to all those other heartbroken parents out there. Having two young boys with an almost six-year gap and different interests was challenging. And there was always that question asked, 'How many children do you have?' How do you answer that? I still struggle even now; it depends what sort of a day I'm having.

December 2002

'We have arrived at a diagnosis of Autism Spectrum Disorder.'

Ohhh. I had heard of autism, chatted with other mums who had children that seemed to be 'different' somehow. But not my Sam? After everything we have been through already? This took me down a new road; a different kind of grief. When your child is diagnosed with a lifelong impactful disability and you are already living through what feels like a bit of a nightmare, actually, you start to grieve for their 'normal' childhood.

Aged 27, I had separated from his dad, we had faced more than our fair share of tests and had a really tough year, and I now had a new partner on the scene. I lived alone with the boys, working part-time and tearing my hair out on a daily basis. Life just kept on throwing challenges at me. I didn't really feel I was in control of my life in any way, and now this? What the hell does it all mean, apart from constant calls home from school, crazy heart-stopping behaviours, and worry for what his future would hold?

Out of somewhere, I found it in me never to give in! We

experimented with diet intervention, which did seem to make a difference. Maybe it bought us a few years which might have been worse without it? The calls home from school were constant, I was struggling to settle down with my now fiancé who found his own selfish release, and I had no energy for anything. Yet I managed to get myself a college qualification in floristry (maybe it was my therapy, some form of escapism, too?). It still presented itself as a series of unanswerable questions, though – is this what was going to shape my life?

December 2005

'You're not pregnant, the symptoms aren't real. I'm sorry, the lining of your womb is so thin it's doubtful you'll conceive for a very long time.'

April 2006

'We took some bloods at your dating scan and we've had the results back. You need to begin treatment immediately – can you get to hospital this morning?'

My head was spinning. Ten years after Jay was taken from me with 'no apparent cause', they had now discovered I have 'sticky blood'. I'm ten weeks pregnant again, with my now husband's first child. His selfish actions in the earliest weeks had made me think I would be doing the whole thing alone, and I should have told him to pack his bags then! My stress levels were already sky high, and now this! What the actual fuck?

I couldn't believe it, but it also felt like a gift from Jay. I wouldn't have to go back to those days of 1997, not knowing anything from one day to the next. They now had an actual medical reason to intervene, they were trying to keep my baby safe, and they were acting on it. Maybe it would be okay? But I was so scared, too. If you have ever been given the kind of news where they greet you at the hospital, take you to a side room, and give you tea in a bone china cup (this is the NHS we are talking about – it just doesn't happen!), you know it's serious. But it was vital they had found it when they did. I began daily injections which they taught me how to do myself, and took a daily dose of aspirin to keep my blood at an acceptably 'viable' level. Extra scans were booked in – more worry; it was bizarre, but somehow still felt like a safety net. Maybe my husband would step up now?

September 2006

'I can't cope with all the stress. I've told them to stick their job.' You bloody what? I am hanging on by a thread, after months of the unknown, hopefully giving birth to your child in a few days, and *you* can't cope?

Give me strength. I can't do this on my own…

'It's a boy!' Zac was delivered after a very long couple of days, weighing in at 7lbs 14oz and a healthy set of lungs. And breathe!!! I still hadn't written off the idea of having any more, even as I sat on the delivery table being sewn up. It had been quite a traumatic delivery, and at one point I thought they were taking me off to theatre. But we made it, and I still had so much love to give. I was a happy contented mum, with a happy contented babe, and life was sweet.

Within a few months of being a mum to my boys, I realised I was done putting myself through all this. It was as if I had more than enough lessons to keep on learning, with Sam and his challenges, Kieran a teenager finding his way in the world, and now one in nappies. It was time to live! To be honest, though, it didn't take long before I felt I was just accepting my lot. Being a mum is incredible; being a wife was hard work. Was it supposed to be that difficult? I constantly questioned everything. Did everyone live like this, constantly striving to find the happy medium in what was supposed to be a partnership?

After many tests and challenges, in December 2014 everything changed, when an argument went horribly wrong and I soon found myself a single mum again. This time, I didn't feel strong. I was broken and worn down, but I knew I had already faced my most difficult tests in life and survived. There was no fucking way I was gonna let some excuse for a man reduce me to this!

I hadn't come this far, to only come this far.

October 2016

A feeling I can only describe as euphoria swept over me as I took control of my life at last. A journey of self-care, self-love, and self-acceptance. A decision to finally live a life I chose. This beautiful awakening would lead me to my soulmate – my one true love and real life Happy Ever After.

July 2017

Our paths were destined to cross, exactly when they did, and even at the ripe old age of 42, we both knew we were made for each other – two halves of a perfect whole. We fell completely head over heels in a matter of days; it was as if we'd always known each other.

When I met Bruce, it was like coming home. It's as if there's a whole new level of belonging that I never dreamed of. More than two years later, we are building a stunningly beautiful new world together, a home with my two youngest boys, new business ideas, and a wedding to plan. Ohhh that dreamy proposal, it was magical!

After years of hard times and heartache, I am now living my life to the fullest, properly and healthily. There are no skeletons in our closet. We embrace a full and frank level of honesty about anything and everything, and everything we do we share as equals.

When my heart has spent years feeling broken and beyond repair, it's the kind of fairytale ending I once never dared to imagine. Thank you.

There's a quote that I've seen on social media: 'One day, someone will hug you so tight that all your broken pieces will fit back together.' For me, that describes our love… and it was definitely worth the wait!

A message to my younger self…

If I could go back in time and speak to my younger self, I'd want to tell her that however hard this is (I don't believe in the word seems, because the pain is very real), and however much pain she is going through right now, it won't always be this tough to face the day. She will still face challenging times, but trust that she will live to fight another day. Her grief is not the only way to remember him.

I wish I had known that by facing the most painful days of my life head-on, I would be stronger in years to come, because nothing else could ever make me feel that empty again.

Being able to survive everything I went through showed me that however much shit life throws at you, you always have a choice. You can choose to be sad forever, or you can face the darkest days and know that your grief is not something to be scared of; you will come through this.

It has taught me that although my heartache will shape who I am to become, it will not define me.

I now feel that my beautiful son Jay was sent to me as a gift. I never believed that at the time – of course I didn't. Losing him at such a young age was truly the hardest lesson, but it has given me as a person a strength I never imagined, to continue through life from the point of view that I have already survived the worst days of my life. I remember him always, in so many ways, and as part of my world every day. But I no longer worry that he will be forgotten. I have got my life back, and after almost two decades of wondering what the point of it all was, I am now at peace with it. He is and always will be my son, and I will always be his mum. A mother's love can never be denied.

If you are going through a similar time right now, please believe me when I say your baby/babies or child will never be forgotten. You will have dark days, but you have already made it this far. Remember to be patient with yourself, be kind to yourself – you can't rush this process. It feels like you will grieve forever, but there will come a time when you are remembering with love; it will come, I promise you. Go through your emotions, don't avoid them, and try not to waste your precious energy on being mad at those who don't understand – you need your energy to recover (please note, that is not a way of saying get over it; there is no such thing!).

I am a woman who shines her beacon of light for those who are finding their way through the darkest days, whatever they may be.

I am The Girl Who Refused to Quit.

Dedication

To Bruce: Thank you for switching the light at the end of the tunnel on for good. I love you.

About the Author

Jacqueline, who lives in Nottingham, England, has been described as a sparkling soul who lights up the room. She is often found looking thoughtful, pen in hand. When she isn't writing, Jacqueline is always creative, spending time with her soulmate Bruce, maybe singing, dancing, or perhaps being silly, and loves family time, too. Jacqueline has dedicated a lot of time to her own personal development and is now simply reaping the rewards. Her mission is to help others see that there is always a light at the end of the tunnel, no matter what challenges they face.

Contact

To find out more about Jacqueline's journey you can find her memoirs on Amazon: https://www.amazon.co.uk/Onward-Upward.../dp/191642581X

Instagram: https://www.instagram.com/jacqueline_e_author/

Facebook: https://www.facebook.com/Jacqueline.E.Author/

Escaping Bohemia

Sophia Moseley

The sound of laughter and love drifted past us, piercing my heart deeper with each minute that passed and with each tear that my little sister shed. I felt helpless, useless, dark, and generally wishing for the floor to swallow up my stupid pointless being. As her big sister and protector, I could do nothing to ease her distress or stop what had occurred earlier that day. I always thought it was my fault, for not trying harder, being better, being more. I was always to blame! We sat there on the cold, hard kerb outside her school at the end of the school day, when most children were filling the air with screams of laughter, not sobs of pure pain. But this was happening, and this hurt was only going to increase with each day that passed.

My little sister adored our mum; she was her shadow and yearned for her love and affection, as any child does. She had not yet realised that the life we lived was not the same as each child that was now passing us, happily skipping off with their mothers to have a nutritious dinner that had been lovingly prepared, and to play with their toys in a safe and caring home.

Instead, I was telling my sensitive little sister, who was

still so small, that our mum was not coming home today and we wouldn't see her for a while because she had been taken to prison that morning, and once again we were all alone. Ok, there were people stepping in, but we were alone – not with the one person in the world that should be there to protect us. That feeling hung around for years. The one person who should always be there for us wasn't then, nor on many other occasions. Can you imagine what damage that causes to a child?

My sweet sister cuddled into me as if we were at home, not sitting in the gutter. She held me with the fear of a small child when losing those they love and need. We knew what came next. She would be palmed off to some kind person, while our mum paid the price for whatever crime was committed this time. It wasn't the first time and certainly wouldn't be the last; we knew that! She had 'been on holiday' a few times at least – that's what we called a stint inside. Somehow that made it nicer, easier to bear – well, for my mother anyway. And to be fair, it probably was a holiday for her. She could hide from many of her demons and the people who made them worse.

It wasn't a holiday for us, though. As much as life at home was difficult, it's where we always came back to and felt safe together. And for us, two innocent impressionable girls, it was another embarrassment, another blow, and more proof. Proof that WE were not a 'normal' nice family. In reality, when my sister went to stay in different homes, the change was nice, beneficial, and the normality was much needed for a little girl who just wanted to be a child, loved and protected. Each child in this world deserves that. Don't you agree?

It's strange that not one adult stopped that day to ask if we needed help or what was wrong. It was one of those times when you feel truly invisible. I'm sure you have experienced that. Two girls crying and holding each other, sitting on the floor, while other 'human beings' carried on as if we were not there, making our feelings of worthlessness even more ingrained into our little souls. Not one person showed any kindness, concern, or acknowledgement. However, I now thank you fellow mums (as I'm now a mum to two fabulous girls). It taught me to always show concern for others in need and never to walk on by, expecting someone else to step in!

My mum was well known on our estate, so probably the thought of those passing adults was, 'Oh, another drama, we best stay away from that!'

Even though we lived on a council estate and it was full of normal working-class folk, as well as those that didn't mind a bit of law-breaking, we were certainly looked down upon for several reasons. It cut me to the core that I felt beneath those around me, and this was something that stayed with me for years. I had to work hard to remove that thought from my head and heart. 'The council estate kid, with a drunk criminal for a mother'.

I gave myself that title and I held it close to my heart, until one day I thought, *F!@# this!, this is not who I am!*

That afternoon, though, we sat outside Oxford Road School until the last of the happy families had disappeared back to their perfect homes...

'Where am I going?' she asked in her quiet voice. She was such a loving, generous child who just loved everyone. All I wanted to do was protect her and look after her, but I couldn't. That guilt stayed with me for many years, that I as the elder child couldn't protect her and give her a better life.

My sister went to stay with one of mum's friends that time; she would do the rounds over the years – friends, family in Norfolk, her father. And in her older years, she spent time with a foster family. I know that I didn't see a great deal of her, and certainly not as much as I would have liked. I felt extreme guilt for not being able to care for her myself, but I was told that I was too young. That is ironic, as I had been caring for her for most of her little life.

For me, the maddest thing happened. I got to stay in our flat, on my own. I think I was about 15, maybe. My father and stepmother didn't want me living with them – and I wouldn't have gone there in a million years, anyway. The last time had been so awful that I certainly didn't want to return, thank you very much. I felt unworthy and a low life as it was, so I didn't need those who were meant to care for me make this feeling more ingrained in my young mind.

As it was a relatively short sentence that time – I think about three months – I was able to stay where I was, so my mum had somewhere to return to when she came out and we would still have a family home. My father and his wife were to keep an eye on me, make sure I was safe, fed, and behaving myself. I still can't understand how this was allowed, or if anyone ever knew about it. Maybe the powers-to-be had no idea, who knows?

Well, guess what? They didn't check on me, not really. Out of sight, out of mind!

'Everything fine?' is all I got in passing.

I saw them on a Friday evening. It was the night that my grandparents visited them, so it made visiting my father's home a little more tolerable, and I went to collect my child maintenance from my dad, which was… wait for it, £5! He had been giving me the money for a little while to stop my mum drinking it away. I think she could only get two bottles of sherry with that, even back in the '80s. I, of course, spent it on food – or probably sweeties.

So, I stayed in our flat on my own for the duration of my mother being on her *holidays*. I thought it was so cool, at first. I really wasn't a party girl, but I had a couple of great friends who stayed over. Boys tended to stay away from me. I thought it was because I was ugly and weird, but I think it may have had more to do with the talks that my mum would give any boy that came near me. She would scare the absolute shit out of them, and normally she would be totally pissed so the whole experience would be a hundred times worse for the poor victim. Of course, she would forget about this little scene, and the next time she encountered the poor boy, she would either be super-nice or start all over again. Hence, no chance of a teenage pregnancy for me. Thanks, Mum – and I really mean that!

So, even though I thought I was some kind of cosmopolitan kid, living in my own apartment, truth be told I was lonely, afraid, sad, and extremely angry with everyone around me. I felt abandoned, unwanted, and unlovable, once again. *Would I ever be wanted?* This thought constantly went through my mind. I actually didn't want to be strong all the time. I wanted someone to care for me, not to just think or say, 'Sophie will be ok, she's strong.'

It's lucky that by this point I had already learned so many unconventional ways to live, eat, and survive. They are all methods that I certainly would not encourage my own beautiful daughters to use and which I have not had to participate in for over 30 years, thankfully. However, I am grateful that as a child, who only had myself to depend on, I had these skills.

For a while, my life was bittersweet whilst she was away. Usually, our flat was full of the kind of people most mothers want their kids to stay away from. So, at least there was respite from that, as well as criminal activities, drink, drugs, and the cruel words that use to flow from her mouth when she was drunk. I started to live and find out who I was and what I wanted in life. This may have been the first time the thought entered my mind that I didn't need to be like 'her'. That I didn't need to end up like these people who so regularly visited our home but never brought any love or happiness. All they seemed to bring was black clouds, negativity, and more pain.

However, I missed my mum, in a way. I was still a child, and even though she hadn't been a mum for years, really, she was still my mother and should have been my protector. I was holding onto those last moments because I knew times and myself were changing and this madness wouldn't always surround me.

I missed my little friend, my sister, tremendously. I had always adored her, so being away from her was extremely hard for me to bear and I cried a lot. I wanted her life to be so different from mine growing up. I wanted her to have a childhood. I didn't want her to encounter the people or activities that I had as I grew into a young woman. I wanted her to have a chance of love, safety, and security. That's probably why I supported my stepfather's application for custody of her, which in hindsight, in my opinion, was a dire mistake. And it was another childhood mistake that I carried a lot of guilt for. But I was a child, and a child without the guidance that I needed.

Even though the flat was full to the brim with other people's things, with other people's history, it always felt empty. It was like an empty box and I was just rolling around in it, waiting. I feared the nights, I feared noises, I feared people, and I was petrified about what could happen if people found out I was there alone. I was literally totally alone.

The other side of the coin was that I started to make my own choices about things as simple as clothes, friends, activities, and food. I still had no idea about cooking a proper meal, but I tried. My good friend from school came to stay some days, and it was a great experience for me to share my space with someone as warm and crazy as she was. She helped me start to learn that 'normal' isn't always so 'normal', and I mean that in the nicest way. I began to feel that I could express myself, be it verbally, in the way I dressed, or what I ate. My mother always had a comment to enlighten me to what I was doing wrong, so it was great not to experience that for a while. Constant criticism is a certain self-esteem killer, and it stops any type of positive progress or growth.

It was during this spell that I went to visit my mum as she was in a local prison, which she had 'visited' a few times before. East Sutton Park is still there today and is set in the most beautiful surroundings. I remember that one of my mum's best friends, Ross, took me to see her. I can't recall if we drove or took the bus; knowing Ross, we probably went by taxi, as he was no doubt pissed! Ross was a very flamboyant character, and my mother adored him and he adored her. By this point in my life, as I developed into a young woman, he normally treated me with disdain and liked to make me feel uncomfortable, which my mum found hysterical.

The thing that I remember most about the prison was the huge dark wooden doors; they were so imposing for a nervous teenager. Those colossal oak doors are etched on my mind, and what was just a physical barrier to my mum back then now appear in my mind when I think about how distant she always was to me. There was always a barrier, something she was locked behind.

However, it was like a stately home rather than somewhere to keep wrongdoers. It really seemed like a holiday camp, with the prisoners wandering around the grounds, laughing and chatting, enjoying the splendour of this gorgeous manor house.

My mum seemed sober, but really, who could tell? She had always been very slim. I think it was from being malnourished as a child, and then as an adult, with the choice between food or alcohol, booze always won hands down. Being in there, she had gained some weight, which she put it down to the doughnuts they made. I had never seen her eat a doughnut in my life, so they must have been good! She made several 'special friends' during her little spells in the holiday camps, which first began when she was about 19 years old. I guess by this point, it felt like a home from home.

I did feel sad for my mum, for being in prison, even though she actually looked quite well. And the building looked absolutely wonderful, like something out of a period drama not out of *The Bill*. But on the other hand, I felt deep rage and bitterness. Why couldn't she get her life sorted out? Why didn't she love us enough to stop with her addictions and all this crime? And why were we always punished by her behaviour? I often wondered why our lives were like that. But I never received an answer.

Ultimately, I just wanted her to be my mum; that's all I have ever wanted. Even now, I long to have a mum to help when times are tough, and just to be held and loved by a woman who loves me for who I am.

Ross and my mum were as animated as ever that day, laughing, chatting and cracking jokes, normally at other people's expense. And I wasn't immune from their unkindness, either. It was only as I grew into an adult that I started to understand why those around me would ridicule me as a teenager, as I started to develop and mature. I use the word mature rather loosely, as I didn't really mature and I certainly wasn't very womanly. However, I was an easy target for those that wanted to share a little spiteful joke. My lack of growth was probably because of my irregular and strange eating patterns as a kid. It's only as I have reflected seriously on those times that I realise certain elements of my childhood have had such an impact on my whole bloody life!

Don't get me wrong, not always in a bad way. Believe me, every cloud does have a silver lining... if you look a little bit deeper!

I spent the brief visit opposite my mum, looking around

in nervous awe. All these women were like my mother. They were all separated from their children, who were sitting across from them. It was one of the first moments that I realised I wasn't the only child with a dysfunctional childhood. There were many tears shed in that room, and the emotion was sorrowfully tangible.

As we left, I saw deep sadness in my mum's eyes. I don't know if it was sorrow because I was leaving, and she loved me. Was she sorry? Did she love me? Or was it because she couldn't take much more of prison? For all the elements that were surprisingly pleasant, it could also be brutal. When she came home, I heard her speak with her friends about drink, drugs, violence, and abuse inside.

She tried hard in prison to stay much more sober, as she wanted to stay in control of herself in situations that could be potentially dangerous. This hurt me for some time, because I wondered why she couldn't do the same on the outside, for the sake of her children. At the time, and for some time after, it was just another reinforcement that she didn't love me. I now know that the situation was a lot more complex than that.

As the heavy wooden doors of the prison slowly shut behind us, I pushed back the tears that were welling up inside my fragile form; by fragile, I mean that I was at breaking point. I was a teenager dealing with hormones, self-doubt and loathing, as well as the loss of my mum and sister. The turmoil of my so far short life had taken its toll on me. I was lost, broken, and alone as a young teen.

By this point in my life, I had learned that crying solved nothing, it just made you vulnerable to those that would use you. I definitely wouldn't receive any sympathetic words from Ross, and don't even mention the word hug! He would have fallen about laughing if I'd said I needed comfort. Then he would have proceeded to tell me to stop making a scene and pull my socks up.

That time in my young life certainly impacted me for a long time after, as did many other experiences. That feeling of loneliness never really left. It was the beginning of the end of my relationship with my mum, and the end of whatever childhood I had left. Even though we had never had the conventional mother-daughter relationship by any stretch of the imagination, the loss hurt. And if I'm truthful, it continues to do so. It was on that day that I knew I had to escape as soon as I could. I had to get out of that environment and stay out, or fast forward 20 years and it might be my daughter visiting me, so the circle would continue!

Always one to go against the grain, I thought, *F@#★ that, I'm not ending up here!*

And I broke that shitty, life-sapping, soul-destroying evil circle!

A message to my younger self...

If I could go back in time and speak to my younger self, I'd want to tell her, sweet child, know now that you are stronger than you believe you are, and your strength will carry you and others through times of darkness. No-one will ever be able to take away your strength, resilience or determination; not one living person has that power; that is your power and yours alone.

Remember that whatever unkindness is uttered from the mouths of those around you, it is their truth, not yours. You do not need to carry the burden of their ugly beliefs, because you are beautiful, inside and out. Your mind is full of delightful, insightful knowledge which you will use to live your fullest, most abundant life.

Embrace your true self. Feel free to follow your path; your dreams are yours. The fire that burns inside you is yours, and it is yours for a reason. No-one has the right, now or in the future, to squash your views, beliefs or dreams… because they are yours and you have a right to hold them close to your heart.

Wear the funky, bright coloured clothes that make your heart sing. Dance to the music that brightens your soul. Write the stories that sing in your heart, and follow YOUR passions. Yes, you are crazy, but all the most wonderful people are. You are in great company!

Take this truth and hold it close to your heart; you are a bright, shining miracle. You may have started behind other children, the climb for you may be steeper, you may have more darkness to break through, BUT – and hear this – you are not beneath anyone. You are equal to all that you come across in your life. You have no reason to feel shame, disgust or hate towards yourself. In fact, you should feel great pride in yourself, because you have survived; you have risen where many have fallen and perished.

Dear Sophie, you ARE loved and cherished because of your sweet, caring, and inspirational spirit. You should never feel that you need to change or hide from who you are or where you come from. Being open about your journey will free you from its bonds. Those that do not understand or believe your words, feel your pain or stand by you, are those that deserve no room in your heart or mind.

Don't give those that don't deserve it a space in your life or mind. Say goodbye quickly and with joy to those that do not see your worth. When they lose you, it's their loss.

Remember, life is an adventure full of joy... and it's yours for the taking. YOU can do anything that you put your mind to! You've made it this far... anything is possible!

'Choice is one of your greatest weapons.'

I'm now grabbing every opportunity that comes by me with both hands and guiding my life to fulfil my dreams, because it's never too late and I deserve that! At last, I've become myself and I'm embracing and loving every PART of ME.

I am a powerful woman, full of resilience, talent, intuition, intelligence, and compassion.

I am The Girl Who Refused to Quit.

Dedication

For my beautiful sweet sister. Together, we survived... thank you.

About the Author

Sophia is a warm-hearted soul who has the determination and resilience of a lioness.

She has travelled through life, with all of its ups and

downs, always knowing that she would come out the other side stronger and wiser.

She is in the process of writing her childhood story, in the hope that her experiences and triumphs will encourage others to keep pushing through the darkness and aim for something better.

Sophia is also a creative portrait photographer, telling other people's stories through her craft.

Sophia lives in her home county of Kent, but is always looking for a travelling adventure.

Contact

www.facebook.com/shutterhut
www.instagram.com/shutterhut
www.linkedin.com/sophiamoseley
www.shutterhutphotography.co.uk
To find out more information about her forthcoming book,
   Escaping Bohemia, you can contact her here.
sophia@shutterhutphotography.co.uk

Is This the End?

Cassandra Farren

August 2019

You stupid cow! How could you do this? You call yourself the girl who refused to quit, yet you've decided enough is enough and you've finally given up. Did you honestly think you had what it takes to succeed? Setting up a business as a single parent with no money, no experience, and no bloody clue what you were doing. What the hell were you thinking? You're an idiot, a complete bloody failure. You've worked your arse off for the last six years for what? Absolutely nothing. You wanted to make a difference. You wanted to make your children proud. All you've done is made a fucking fool of yourself!

As I sat on the edge of my bed, crying so hard that I couldn't catch my breath, there was one question spinning around in my head. Why? Why the hell did I bother in the first place? Why did I listen to the words that changed my life in 2012?

Having ended my marriage and been at one of the lowest points in my life, I'd taken my friend's advice and booked a coaching call with an intuitive lady who I was told was amazing at giving guidance.

Have you ever had a conversation with someone

who believed in you more than you believed in yourself? Someone who gave you hope when you felt that all was lost? After pouring out everything that had occurred in my life, this is exactly what happened to me. Her response stunned me into silence…

'The reason that your career hasn't worked out is because you were never meant to be under someone else's umbrella. You're so much more inspiring than you realise, Cassie. I want you to write down everything that has happened in your life, and everything will become apparent.'

Why didn't I phone a friend and talk it through? Why, oh why, did I take her advice and write it down? Why didn't I do what normal people do – get a job, have a job description, and have a salary? Oh my God, a salary! I could barely remember what that felt like.

I'm still not sure how I did it, but three months after that call I set up my business with nothing more than a Facebook page and a temporary overdraft. I continued to write my life story, and two years later – against all the odds – I published my first book, *The Girl Who Refused to Quit.*

I was under no illusion that my life would magically transform and that I'd retire off the royalties, but I also didn't expect my life to collapse for the third time just one year later. The shit hit the fan in a big way. But despite my world falling apart, I didn't. This experience inspired me to publish my second book, *Rule Your World – Reduce Your Stress, Regain Your Control, Restore Your Calm.* A few months later, I was asked to host a Facebook Live on how to write a book. I had big imposter syndrome, but agreed and decided to give it my best shot! I was then inundated with comments and messages from people telling me how much my journey from a cleaner to becoming an author had inspired them, and did I offer mentoring for authors? Err… give me a few days and I will!

I created an author mentoring programme and decided to turn this into my third book, which was published six months later, *Share Your World – how to write a life-changing book in 60 days*.

You may be thinking: *Wow! You published three books. Your life must be pretty sorted*. Actually, I was holding it together by a thread. Whilst all of this was going on, I was not only bringing up my two boys on my own whilst running my business and working two freelance jobs, but I had also been trying to cope with the hardest challenge of my life – my mum having advanced dementia. Just 19 days after publishing *Share Your World*, I started to write my fourth book; 28 days later, the first draft of *I've Lost My Mum* was finished. I cried, and I cried, and I cried! Reliving my pain and trauma was almost unbearable, but I had a deep knowing that our story needed to be shared.

In May 2019, I published *I've Lost My Mum*. It received an overwhelmingly positive response, but I would still look at the cover with my mum fading away and weep. Yes, I was proud that our journey was making a difference but, my God, I wished it wasn't our journey. Speaking at my book launch at Mum's care home was heartbreaking. There are no words to describe the feeling of knowing that my mum was downstairs, not knowing that I'd published another book or even that I was her daughter. No matter how challenging things are, I am very good at finding a positive, and this was no different.

When my mum went into the care home, her condition went downhill so rapidly that I had to have an honest conversation with my children, Kieron and Lennie (aged 15 and 9), and ask them a question that no mother should ever have to ask: Would they prefer to visit their nana knowing that she wouldn't know who they were and lie to her to keep her happy, or would they prefer never to see her again? They both decided not to see my mum and to remember her as she was. But on her birthday a few months later, Lennie changed his mind and we had a very positive visit, which ended up with me and my mum dancing to her favourite song, *Dancing Queen,* for over an hour!

Both of the boys came to my book launch, and I told them that after my talk I wanted to see my mum and give her a copy of my book. I said they didn't have to come and were welcome to wait in the reception. After my talk, Lennie came up to me and said, 'Mum, guess what? Kieron has decided to come and see Nana, too!' Once again, we had a positive visit with a happy Nana. Despite not knowing who her grandchildren were, she was laughing, smiling and, yes, you guessed it, dancing to *Dancing Queen*!

As we drove home, the sun was setting. I felt proud that due to writing my book the boys had got to see their nana happy again.

I took on some new one-to-one mentoring clients. Momentum was building, and I had a knowing that I needed to take the next step in my business. I wanted to offer my authors the option to publish their book through my own publishing company. I had set up Welford Publishing in 2014, but until now I had only published my own books. It was a big step, but it would be amazing to not only help these authors to write a life-changing book, but to publish one, too.

Shit, shit, shit! With my big girl pants on, I e-mailed my accountant and told her I'd like to set up Welford Publishing Limited. I then posted on my Facebook page that Welford Publishing Limited was in progress. And that was when everything started to go pear-shaped…

Summer holidays were hard. You may have seen hundreds of Facebook posts from mothers around the world #livingtheirbestlife, as they effortlessly juggle six weeks of working combined with a lovely holiday and endless days out. Not me. Yes, I'm proud that I haven't had to pay a childminder since setting up my business. But my goodness, completing the same amount of work in half the amount of time, feeling guilty if I'm working, feeling guilty if I'm not is blimmin' tough! I felt drained. I was already on a slippery slope downhill, but what happened next sent me sliding into the dark in a big way.

This was the beginning of the end. This was the situation that made me question everything. This was the catalyst for destruction that lead to my next two actions:
1) I sent an e-mail to my accountant, asking her to put Welford Publishing Limited on hold.
2) I uploaded my CV online and began my search for an employed job.

I had had enough. Enough of the pressure. Enough of the bullshit. Enough of people taking the piss. I was done. There was nobody that could say I hadn't given this my all. I had lost count of the amount of times I'd been told I'd made a difference to someone's life, but I didn't have anything left to give.

You may be wondering if you've missed something. What on earth happened to lead to this? If you have read my other books, you'll know that I never share the *actual* shit that goes on 'behind the scenes'. Why? Because it's not about *them;* it's about my challenges and how I have overcome them.

Fast forward two weeks and I had applied for over 20 jobs, full time, part time, permanent and temporary. When asked about why I was seeking a new position, I was honest and said that I wanted stability in my life. Maybe I was naïve to think that I could do this on my own without any support? But despite the many obstacles I had faced, I still believed that I had something to give the world, something that was needed. This was never just my business; this was my purpose.

This was why I broke down in tears after the following conversation:

'Hello, can I speak to Cassandra Farren?'

'Hi, yes that's me.'

'Are you still interested in the job as the evening cleaner?'

Am I interested?! No, I bloody well am not interested! But this is what my life has come to and I'm not too proud to do whatever it takes to put food on the table – is the answer my head was screaming! The answer that came out of my mouth, however, was:

'Yes, I am. Could you tell me more about the role and the hours?'

I hung up the phone in shock. Was this actually happening? I'd just agreed to go into the job agency to register the next day. Part of me was devastated, but another part of me did not give a shit! I had well and truly surrendered; the flame within me had gone. Maybe I'd helped the people I needed to help and it was now time for my life to go back to normal?

But the anger inside me was still building. If my life's purpose was to be a cleaner, then why the hell didn't I just stay in my dead-end job and clean toilets for the rest of my life? Why had I had to endure the hardest six years of my life, constantly making sacrifices and surviving against all odds? Why had I fought time and time again to end up back where I started, and feeling like a complete failure?

I walked into the job agency feeling like a zombie. I filled out a million and one forms stating why I was the best cleaner for the job. I asked what happened next, not really wanting to know the answer. I was told my details would be sent to the company, I'd receive a call to confirm, and could I start on Monday?

Monday? That was only three days away. I walked into a clothes shop, bought two t-shirts (aka my new cleaning uniform) and resigned myself to the fact that this was not a false alarm. It was 100% over. Now all I needed to do was to have the two conversations I was dreading…

'Kieron, just to let you know I've applied for a job as a cleaner. I'm waiting for a call to confirm, but it looks like I'm starting on Monday. It means we'll be having dinner early and I won't be back until 8.30pm each day.'

'Ok. A cleaner? What happened to being an author and making a difference in the world?'

'Honestly? I don't know. I tried my best, but it seems it wasn't meant to be.'

★

'Lennie, I've got some good news and some bad news. The bad news is that I'm going to working every evening as a cleaner. The good news is that I can still take you to school and pick you up each day. I'm sorry that it's come to this.'

'That's ok, Mum, it's not the end of the world.'

My boys never cease to amaze me at how well they cope with change, but it didn't stop me feeling like a really crap mum.

Anyone who asked me if I was ok got the honest answer that I wasn't ok, but I wasn't fighting any more. If this was meant to be, then so be it.

Monday came. The agency didn't call. Maybe the paperwork was delayed? Tuesday came. The agency didn't call. Maybe my business prayers had been answered, but in the meantime I had another challenge to deal with.

Most of the time, I cope surprisingly well with my mum's dementia, but there are times when I feel anxious, emotional, and angry for no apparent reason. I know now that this is referred to as living grief, but it's not commonly recognised as my mum's still alive. All of these emotions came to the surface on my mum's birthday in September. Lennie asked if he could come and see my mum again, and I prayed that we would have another positive visit. But it seems my prayers weren't heard, as it was a complete disaster from start to finish.

My mum was not in a good mood and completely ignored Lennie; she didn't say one word to him or even look at him. She was more concerned with the imaginary man who she immediately needed to find. I know and understand that this is not my mum, this is the dementia.

I also know that she loves my son to bits, but when you're standing in an empty corridor with your mum who is angry and fixated on finding an imaginary man whilst your son is looking sad and disheartened, it's no wonder that sometimes it all gets too much. A few years earlier, we would have all been celebrating whilst laughing, joking, and having fun together. Then I could have also told my mum that I was having a hard time, and she would have told me she was proud of me and she'd support me in whatever I decided. But not any more. She didn't know who I was or that my life was hanging by a thread.

We eventually managed to get my mum into the garden where she ate some cake whilst we played *Dancing Queen*. I could tell Lennie didn't feel comfortable, so after 30 minutes we left. I drove home feeling empty, sad, and alone. Not only was I grieving for my mum, but I was also grieving for my children's nana. It's times like this when I just want a hug and for someone to tell me it's going to be ok.

A few days later, I was aimlessly scrolling through my Facebook feed when I saw that a business coach, Julie Creffield, was launching a new challenge. It sounded great, but I felt that low that I ignored it and decided it was too late to turn things around. A week later, 12 hours before the challenge was due to start, I received an email from my friend, Lis Cashin, to say: *Look at this amazing challenge, I'm joining, and you should too!* You guessed it, it was Julie's! Now, despite losing my belief in my business, there was still a part of me that said this was a sign. So, I joined.

I've signed up for lots of business challenges in the past and not seen any results, but right from the start there was something different about the energy of this group. The honesty of over 100 business owners, all admitting that they wanted more, and that was ok.

The challenge was to launch a new product in the next seven days, and to set yourself an income target. Julie told us that we had to be all in, or it wouldn't work. I believed her and decided I had nothing to lose, but what on earth could I launch?

It was later that evening when the words came to me, completely out of the blue. As soon as I heard them, I knew. The spark that had extinguished itself started to very gently flicker. I wasn't going to quit. I was going to give this my all.

I contacted all of the ladies that I had worked with earlier this year. I knew they wanted to share their story but they all felt overwhelmed with writing and publishing by themselves. The vulnerability of baring their souls was holding them back. I confidently told them that I had a solution. I had found a way where we could all stand together and collectively publish a book that would make a difference.

What were the words I heard that night?

The Girls Who Refused to Quit!

What happened next?

The job agency didn't call. It appears the angels had my back!

If you're wondering what happened with my accountant, I e-mailed her and said: *It's all systems go!*

Welford Publishing Limited was incorporated on the 10th of October and already has plans to publish four books from the authors I've mentored:

How to Feel Beautiful – by Lizi Jackson-Barratt

Light after Dark – A true story of love and loss by Vimi Seewooruthun

What the Hell Just Happened? A compelling, true story of how a couple are rebuilding their life after it was shattered by a traumatic brain injury – by Mark and Jules Kennedy

The Girls Who Refused to Quit – by 14 incredible authors, whose stories you have just read!

To be continued…

A message to my younger self...

If I could go back in time and speak to my younger self, I would want to tell her that I'm sorry. I'm sorry that I hated you for making what I thought were the wrong choices. I'm sorry that I didn't feel you were worthy of success, and I'm sorry that I didn't treat you with the love and respect that you deserved.

You are, and always have been, more than enough.

I wish I had known that when you follow your heart it can be a long and painful journey that many people will never understand. You will make decisions that seem illogical, it will take longer than you'd hoped, and you will face many challenges along the way. People who you thought you could trust will betray you. Trust that they are helping you to become even stronger.

You may lose your way and feel like nothing is going to plan. This isn't because you have failed, it's because no-one has ever walked this path before. You are forging your own way. There will be times when you fall off your track and there will be times when others will push you off your track, but never lose sight of your destination or the lessons you have learned along the way.

Being able to survive everything I have been through has shown me that I am a strong and capable woman who is a force to be reckoned with. I didn't just wake up one day with resilience and determination; these foundations were built as a result of the many life challenges I've faced and overcome, many of them alone.

I now feel calm and at peace, despite ongoing challenges in my life. I trust in myself and I feel proud that I have given my life meaning by authentically sharing my journey. I know that through finding my courage I've made a difference to my life as well as to hundreds of others.

I am the girl who followed her heart and followed her dreams.

I am The Girl Who Refused to Quit.

Dedication

For Lis, thank you for being my angel in disguise x

About the Author

Cassandra, who lives in Northamptonshire, England, has been described as 'a gentle soul powered by rocket fuel'!

When she's not working as a ghostwriter, mentoring authors or writing life-changing books, Cassandra can often be found relaxing by a beautiful lake or having a dance party in her kitchen!

She is a very proud Reiki master, who has committed to her own journey of healing and spiritual growth,

Cassandra's mission is to create a new generation of heart-led authors who collectively make a difference in the world, one book at a time.

Contact

www.cassandrafarren.com
Facebook page/ cassandrafarren1
Facebook group/ heartledauthors
To be considered to become an author in a future Welford Publishing collaboration, please e-mail: hello@ cassandrafarren.com

Poem by Cassandra

Your questions have now been answered,
You know the steps to take.
Don't be afraid; be true to yourself;
Have faith, it's not too late.

It's time to replace your tears with smiles,
The best is yet to come.
You've got this chance to live your life,
Your happiness has now begun.

Follow your heart and follow your dreams,
Have courage to take the right path.
Believe in yourself, maintain your pride,
You've already come so far.

Hold your head high, live life on your terms.
You can do this, it's time to commit.
Know that you're worthy, take one step at a time.

From

The Girls Who Refused to Quit

Acknowledgements

I would like to thank all of authors from *The Girls Who Refused to Quit*. I am honoured that you have trusted me to become a part of your journey. Thank you for bravely sharing your stories which I know will empower and inspire so many others.

Thank you to Jamie Scher Drake for intuitively guiding me to find our amazing cover photograph.

Thank you to Guille Álvarez for taking the incredible cover photograph. As soon as I saw the photograph, I felt the uplifting energy. I am so grateful that you captured this special moment with your friends.

Thank you to our editor Christine McPherson. Who would have thought that when you edited *The Girl Who Refused to Quit* that 5 years later you would be editing my fifth book!

Thank you to Jen Parker from Fuzzy Flamingo for typesetting our book and designing our beautiful cover.

The Girl Who Refused to Quit

The Girl Who Refused to Quit tells the surprisingly uplifting journey of a young woman who has overcome more than her fair share of challenges.

When she hit rock bottom for the third time Cassandra was left questioning her worth and her purpose. She could have been forgiven for giving up on everything. Instead she chose to transform adversity into triumph and with not much more than sheer determination Cassandra has now set up her own business to empower other women.

She is the girl who refused to be defined by her circumstances. She is the girl who wants to inspire other women, to show them that no matter what challenges you face you can still hold your head high, believe in yourself and follow your dreams.

She is The Girl Who Refused to Quit.

Rule Your World

Reduce Your Stress, Regain Your Control & Restore Your Calm

Have you ever questioned why your head is in such a mess – even when your life appears to look so good?

You know something needs to change, but don't know where to start?

When she became a single parent for the third time Cassandra feared her head may become a bigger mess than her life and inadvertently began to follow "The Rules".

Sharing her thought provoking and refreshing personal insights Cassandra's 7 rules will help to raise your self-awareness and empower a calmer, more fulfilling way of living.

Combining relatable real-life stories, and intriguing scientific studies with simple but powerful exercises,

you will gain your own "Toolbox for Life" as well as admiration for this determined and strong woman.

Cassandra is living proof that when you reduce your stress, regain your control & restore your calm, you too can Rule Your World.

Share Your World

How to write a life-changing book in 60 days

How many times do you need to be told, "You should write a book" before you finally believe that you could become an author?

Your heart wants to share your story, but your head feels overwhelmed; Where do you find the courage to start, how do you make a plan to ensure you finish, and who would really want to read about your real-life journey?

Cassandra has written a positive and practical guide for aspiring authors, who want to make a difference to the lives of others by sharing their story.

In her natural, relaxed (and brutally honest!) style of writing, Cassandra shares her simple tools and tips whilst letting you into her own inspiring, yet unlikely, story of how she became the author of three books.

Cassandra's uplifting guidance will empower you to Share Your World and write a life-changing book, in only 60 days!

I've Lost My Mum

I've Lost My Mum tells the true, soul-baring, account of a daughter who wants to make a difference to those whose lives have been devastated by dementia.

Cassandra's raw and deeply moving journey shares her own struggle for strength as well as invaluable insights into this invisible illness. This heartfelt and compelling story not only provides a deeper understanding of this cruel condition but gives hope that it's possible to find peace when someone you love is lost between worlds.

Contact Cassandra

www.cassandrafarren.com

Facebook page/ cassandrafarren1

Facebook group/ heartledauthors

To be considered to become an author in a future Welford Publishing collaboration, please e-mail: hello@cassandrafarren.com

Request

If you have enjoyed reading our book, please can you leave a review on Amazon?